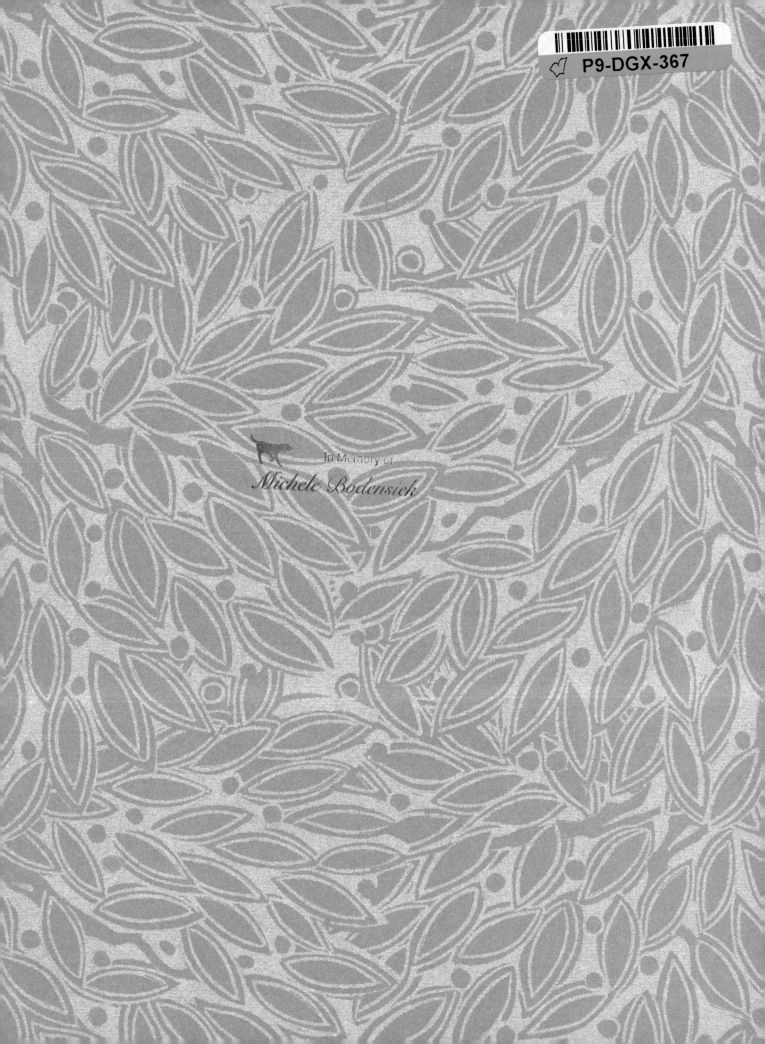

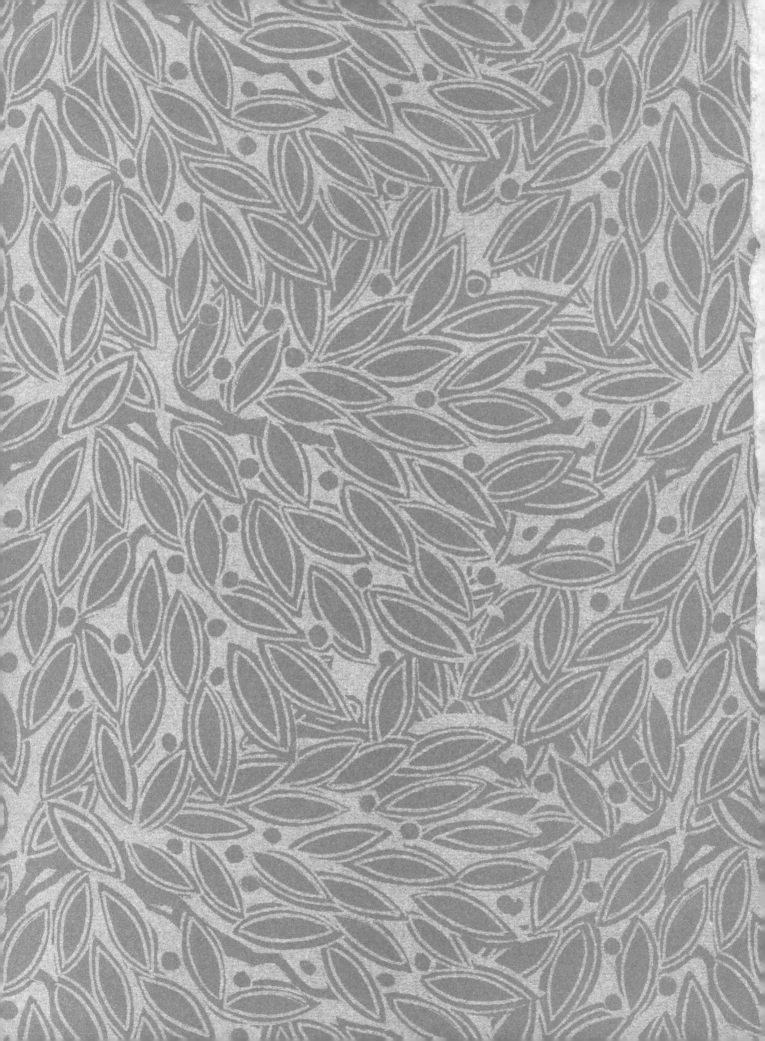

Olive Oil
A Gourmet Guide

OLIVIER BAUSSAN
and JACQUES CHIBOIS

Photographs
by Jean-Charles Vaillant
assisted by
Valérie Lhomme

Flammarion

For Serge Lions
Olivier Baussan

For Michel Guérard, who introduced me
to olive oil with his recipe for steamed bass
à la Vierge

Jacques Chibois

Editor Direction
GHISLAINE BAVOILLOT

Art Director
MARC WALTER/BELA VISTA

Translation
TRACY DANISON

Copy-Editor
BERNARD WOODING

Production
CLAUDE BLUMENTAL

Recipe consultant
ELISABETH DE MEURVILLE

© Flammarion, Paris 2000
ISBN: 2-0801-3676-3
Numéro d'édition: FA 3676
Dépôt légal: March 2000
Printed and bound by
Canale, Italy

Contents

6
Once Upon a Time
There was Olive Oil

80
Jacques Chibois's
Recipes

150
Connoisseur's Guide

Once Upon a Time There was Olive Oil

It may be hard to believe of a man whose childhood horizons were shaped by Provence and its olive groves, but I didn't come to love olive oil on my own. It was the painter of Haute-Provence, Serge Fiorio, who taught me to appreciate it. It's the solemn truth.

Enthusiasts of the Provençal novelist Jean Giono, my parents left Paris in the 1950s for an old farm on the plateau of the ancient Ganagobie Priory, not far from Lurs. Their flight was a search for an authenticity that the flower children were to give full wing in the 1960s back-to-the-land movement. While awaiting the next decade, however, my parents had the heavy work of restoring the farm. Serge Fiorio regularly came down from his village of Montjustin in the Lubéron to lend them a hand.

Serge had acquired his love of the oil from his cousin, my parents' hero Jean Giono himself. It was Serge

who painted the portrait of the writer that now hangs in the museum at Laval. Now nearly ninety, Serge still lives at Montjustin and continues to prepare his own olives. His recipe is simple: he pops them freshly picked into a canning jar, screws the lid and leaves them for twelve months. He only adds the salt and herbs when a jar is opened. Serge's genius in local matters olive is still recognized by friends such as Henri Cartier-Bresson and Pierre Bergé. Pierre never forgets to bring over a sample of his own production.

The writer Pierre Magnan, like Serge, acquired his love of the olive from Jean Giono. But, despite the respect Pierre no doubt owes his teacher, the two men have never been able to agree on the right place to mill the fruits of their labors. Jean has always refused to take his olives anywhere but the Monessargues mill at Lurs. Pierre, whose groves lay in the rolling foothills of Mont d'Or above the town of Manosque, keeps his faith and his custom in that town's cooperative mills.

I have a very clear memory of the winter

Julien Masse, the soul of the Monessargues mill at Lurs,
still helps his niece and her husband (above). Traditional methods are used and the manual work
has remained unchanged for centuries. The oil is skimmed out with the feuille,
a sort of large flat spoon, and strained to remove the suspended particles of crushed olive
in the oil (right). A centenary olive tree in the village of Lurs (pages 6–7).

when Serge Fiorio led my father and I to the Monessargues olive mill. It was the first time I had ever seen an olive mill and it made a big impression on me. Patches of soot covered the walls of the large cave where the mill was located. Two enormous grinding stones turned amid a truly frightening racket while hydraulic mills oozed and groaned, crushing the olives into a paste that was then put on plates of wickerwork (*scourtins*) for pressing. A nearby boiler, beneath which a few embers still glowed, seemed ready to explode. It all seemed alive and took my breath away.

I remained merely fascinated—and a little frightened—up to the moment I noticed the olive oil flowing along the *scourtins* and into large wooden barrels. It seemed impossible that this thick green fluid that smelled so strongly of apple and artichoke could be the result of the obscure process of transformation I was witness to.

After the visit, Serge taught my father the rudiments of olive cultivation. We then began to spend our winter weekends harvesting the olives of the few trees on our farm. My father never stopped doing his business with the cooperative at Lurs, where he often met his hero Jean Giono, and we were never without our own oil on the table.

So while olive oil was a part of my life —as it was, and still is, a part of every Mediterranean life—it was so much a part of my life that I didn't really pay much attention to it. And then I started making my own household soaps using olive oil for Occitane, the cosmetics company I created in 1976 with the idea of using only natural and ecologically sound essences and oils. I was struck by the symbolic power of the olive tree and swore I would find a way of doing it honor one day.

IN DEFENSE OF THE OLIVE TREE

It wasn't until twenty years later that I finally looked again at the olive tree that had been so much a part of my youth. With Marie-Claire Maurin and Christophe Castiglione, two former colleagues at Occitane, and my son Laurent, I plunged into the enormous project of rethinking the cultural and artistic approach to the olive tree. One of the oldest symbols of the Mediterranean world, it is also one of the dowdiest and dustiest.

Imagine: a thousand years of continuous cultivation and not an ounce of innovation, not the slightest questioning of the way we look at the reigning tree of our regions. The olive tree wasn't taboo. It was no secret.

The oil made at Nyons is protected by an Appellation d'Origine Contrôlée.
It is pressed from the Tanche olive, the source of its perfect balance,
and its delicate bouquet of hazelnut and almonds.

On the contrary, everybody talked about it, everybody wanted it ... to plant in the middle of our suburban traffic circles. The olive tree—so deeply rooted in the economic life of most Mediterranean countries—had been reduced to the role of highway decoration. So I decided to try and do something myself to change our way of looking at the olive, its fruits and its products. With Marie-Claire, Christophe and Laurent, I created Oliviers & Co. with the aim of developing a cultural approach to the olive tree.

The first step was to send out twenty photographers of Mediterranean origin to work freely over a year on the theme of the olive tree. We asked Christian Caujolle from the Vu photo agency to help us put the plan into action. A year later we had in hand more than two hundred exceptional and original photographs of the good old olive tree. Some of the photographs show the similarities of gesture and attitudes among olive growers throughout the Mediterranean world, some of whom are separated by thousands of miles.

In addition to asking for pictures, I also asked the photographers to send me bottles of olive oil produced in their own countries. The result is easy to guess, but for me, brought up on the olive oil grown by my father, it was a revelation. I received bottles of dull, pale greens and sun-bright yellows, of opalescent jades, emerald greens and pale yellows, with scents of almond, artichoke, pear and tomato, and flavors which could be sweet, hot or spicy. What a range of tastes! The diversity of colors and scents filled me with the desire to make them available to other lovers of olive oil, so that they too could enjoy the different varieties as they might enjoy the varieties, the *crus*, of wine.

The first person I turned to with my little collection of oils was Elisabeth Scotto, a writer and passionate cook. She immediately created a range of original, tasty dishes to keep us going during the project. From the start we wanted to surround ourselves with the great professional connoisseurs to ensure the right approach.

On advice from my dear friend Jean Lenoir, the creator of the Nez du Vin

These fresh olives (above) are available in the Forville market at Cannes, which is where Jacques Chibois gets his supplies. He prepares them himself before using them in his dishes. The little round Provence goat's milk cheeses slowly take on the savors of the oil and herbs (facing page). They are tasty accompanied by finely sliced pear and good, crusty bread: a gourmet marriage of flavors to mark the end of summer.

and a world-renowned wine taster, we asked Eric Verdier, a peerless specialist in the analysis of taste and smell, to join our project team. His ruthlessly scientific methods stripped, almost literally, each of our oils naked in the search for their secrets, before and after we put them on sale.

Jean-Marie Meulien, a member of Haute-Cuisine Française and former chef at the Oasis restaurant at Napoule and Clos du Longchamp (the restaurant of the Méridien-Etoile Hotel) was also asked to join with us. His long experience in the kitchen and his thorough knowledge of olive oil products has helped us to create our culinary combinations using the ancient fruit and its oil. It was also Jean-Marie who initiated one of the most enriching encounters of our early days when he introduced us to Jacques Chibois, the talented chef at La Bastide Saint-Antoine in Grasse. Jacques has an approach to the kitchen that is both passionate and imaginative. He combines a freshness and generosity of view that protects him from excess and error at the stove.

When Jacques and I met he was enthusiastic about the varieties of oil I introduced him to and set about looking for new ways of giving olive oil a different role in cooking, drawing it out of its traditional low-key role in Provençal cuisine and into new dishes. Because his work seemed so much a part of what I took to be our work, he was asked to take the second part of this book under his wing.

Other chefs now use the oils we have marketed to make their own culinary marvels. Michel del Burgo in Bristol and Alain Passard in Paris, Philippe Da Silva at the Gorges de Pennafort in Callas, the Frères Pourcel in Montpellier, Anne Pic at Valence, Troigros at Roanne and Alain Lamaison from La Carbo d'Or in Baux de Provence. Lamaison has put together a delicious menu in which each dish is seasoned by a different variety of oil. And we mustn't forget Reine Sammut, who features a magnificent *menu de dégustation* he calls "Olive Oils and the Mediterranean" for his Fenière restaurant at Lourmarin, featuring a *St Pierre à la vanille et l'huile d'olive de Curcuron*, a *tomate tartare à la coriandre*

To perfect his recipes, Jacques Chibois (above) tested many olive oil crus,
assessing the results of combinations with a variety of fruits, meats, vegetables and spices,
as well as methods of cooking. Another product of Provence,
the small round goat cheeses enjoyed fresh in spring and summer marry deliciously
with the rather sweet and rounded oils of Nyons or Catalonia (left).

et petit violets au parmesan à l'huile d'olive de Galilée, a *risotto aux truffes blanches à l'huile d'olive d'Istrie,* a *barbue à la moelle et millefeuille croustillant de légumes au basilic à l'huile d'olive de Toscane,* a *râble de lapereau aux pieds de cochons,* an *épaule rôtie et poêlée de champignons à l'huile d'olive de Baena,* a *fromage de chèvre à l'huile d'olive du Péloponnèse* and, even, a *pain perdu à l'huile d'olive de Sardaigne.* A true Mediterranean symphony in olive oil major!

VOYAGE TO THE WORLD OF OLIVE OIL

For more than two years I visited most of the Mediterranean olive-producing countries trying to learn and understand how the olive is grown.

The heartlands of olive cultivation are also the heartlands of the imagination and bounty: Andalusia, Tuscany, Latium, Sicily, Umbria, the Peloponnese, Galilee and Cap Bon. On every shore olive oil has its *crus,* its *grand crus* and its *ordinaires.* If some of these are already well known, many of them remain to be discovered and some even to be reborn.

I didn't start my journey to the world of olives with the idea of trying to find the finest *cru.* Rather, I was careful never to refuse a piece of advice or decline an invitation to a good meal or glass of wine after a visit to the olive groves. Every time I went out, I went out as a trailblazer. My intention was to open up paths for Christophe, who would make our definitive selections with the aid of his technical expertise.

This book is not intended to be the exhaustive reference for olive oils, but rather a trip through the different regions of this remarkable fruit. It is a trip strewn with numerous encounters and thousands of flavors, conducted at a Mediterranean speed, from olive tree to olive tree, from *cru* to *cru.*

THE *CRUS*: A NEW WAY OF LOOKING AT OLIVE OIL

No sooner had I set out on my voyage of discovery than I understood that olive oil, like wine, has its vintages, its *crus.* They are not immutable, as quality varies from

One of the dramatic moments in the birth of a Provençal olive oil (above). Provence in Paris: on the table at La Bastide Odéon, near the Odéon Theater, olive oil from the mill of Jean-Marie Cornille in the Vallée des Baux. Ample in the mouth, the oil has a bouquet of white flowers, bitter almond and pear (facing page).

season to season depending on the weather. Nevertheless, the different *crus* each retain unique, basic characteristics that I rapidly came to recognize.

Until recently, no one had bothered much about the notion of *cru* because olive oil brands had most often been made using olives from a variety of regions. Oils labeled as Spanish, Tunisian and Italian are mixes that are usually sold under an Italian brand name. The provenance of the olives is not always mentioned on the label. The consumer who prefers Italian oil is often getting Spanish oil without knowing it.

Like vines, olive trees vary according to climate and soil conditions. Again, as for vines, olives grown on a plain tend to yield diluted tastes. Olive trees are often grown on hillsides, but will not grow above a certain altitude. They tolerate poor soil, but need water—notably summer rain—to thrive. It is frequently necessary to irrigate and, as I was able to see myself in Andalusia in 1996, a few seasons of drought can bring production down quite radically.

The olive, like the grape, comes in different varieties. Each country has its preferences, usually established over a long period, and these are often based on the fact that a particular variety adapts well to the local soil. Even when a particular variety produces distinctive oils based on regional soil and climate conditions and different methods of milling, it retains a personality that can be distinguished from one *cru* to another. The variety of olive, then, is a good guide, even if many are sisters, cousins, or even identical twins going under different names in different regions.

In museums of olive culture, whether the Guzmann Hacienda near Seville or that of Porquerolles in France, I saw nearly one hundred varieties of olive tree. They all looked very much alike, but each produced quite different fruit in terms of roundness, size and color. Some are thick around the pit, others skimpy, some are smooth while others have spidery wrinkles or are ribbed.

In France I rapidly learned to recognize the Cailletier, the little black olive of the Nice region, which produces a very sweet oil; the Aglandau, an interesting variety, but difficult when it comes to extracting its fruity oil; the Tanche, the Nyons olive, with sweet, milky oil; the Grossane; the Salomenque; the Picholine; the Bouteillan; the Lucques; the Sabina, to name but a few. This is a very large family indeed!

In Spain the Andalusian Picual delighted me with its strong, tasty, vegetal flavor.

The olive is a winter fruit. Green olives are harvested in September and October and black olives from November to February. Pictured here (facing page) from top left to right, the Cayer Roux, Salonenque, Tanche and Lucques varieties.

The Picual has a light aftertaste of bitterness, as does the Catalan Arbequina, which yields a fruity and very fine oil that leaves a lingering hint of bitter almond and spice. I also discovered the Hojiblanca. Its sweet, fresh oil sometimes has a rather animal touch. I still dream of the taste of the Ocal, a very fine table olive which, it seems, also produces a superb oil much praised by a friend of mine from Seville who is a great connoisseur of olives.

In Italy, the Tuscan and Umbrian Frantoios, Moraiolos and Leccinos, whose delicately fruity, slightly grassy taste varies from place to place, are quite well known, but I was also invited to taste the intensely green Sicilian Nocellara de Belice, which has a spicy savor, as well as the Taggiasca from Liguria—a famous, very black little olive close to the French Cailletier and which, like the latter, is harvested very late and gives a very sweet oil.

In Portugal I tasted the Galega, in Greece the Koroneiki and the Kalamata, in Galilee the Souri, the Barnea, the Nabali and the Manzanillo, in Istria the Lecino and the Buga, in Tunisia the Chetoui … each trip that I made revealed a new variety. But it should not be forgotten that a given oil is rarely the product of a single variety. Rather, it is a blend—sometimes carefully calculated, sometimes almost random— of different varieties, the success of which varies. Many mixes are forced marriages of tradition, which, I am pleased to say, contemporary research sometimes calls into question.

Of course, cultivation techniques play their role in the quality of the product. The great enemy of the olive tree is the olive fly. Keeping it at bay requires a twice-yearly treatment with a concoction of copper sulfate, usually in February and August. As I saw in numerous countries, if the trees are not treated, the fly attacks, putting the oils in jeopardy or even rendering them inedible.

The age of the trees affects the quantity of olives produced, but not the quality. An olive tree starts fruiting at from eight to ten years old and produces fully to about one hundred years old. After its centenary,

Olives all look alike for the neophyte, but the experienced eye has learned to recognize them (facing page, top left to right, the Cailletier, Picoline, Cayon, Bouteillan varieties; above, the Grossane). Returning from the Moulay Idriss Market in Morocco. *This photograph was taken for the exhibition "Olivier, Arbre de l'Unité," organized by Oliviers & Co., along with twenty others by Mediterranean photographers working freely on the themes of the olive tree and olive oil (following double page).*

the tree's productivity declines. I have seen, however, especially in certain parts of the Peloponnese, centuries-old trees producing impressive quantities of olives.

The date and handling of the harvest have a very important role in determining olive oil quality. Harvesting lasts about three months, from around mid-November to the end of February. The right time to harvest depends on the variety of olive involved. In the Nice region, the harvest is later than elsewhere, taking place in January or February, because the Cailletier variety takes a long time maturing to the point where it produces a good oil. It is therefore imperative to find the right date for harvesting each olive variety according to local conditions.

I was able to see a link between early harvesting and good-quality oil: as the fruit matures the acidity responsible for sourness increases, while the phenols—natural "preservatives" of the oil—decrease. In general, oils produced from olives harvested early, when they are "turning"—that is to say still green with just a shade of violet—and not yet fully matured, are a lovely green (the more mature the olive, the more the oil is yellow and sweet) and have a strong and fruity flavor. However, these young olives, being firmer and less fleshy, produce less oil.

Picking also has its effects. As for other fragile fruits, hand-picked olives lightly tossed into a basket are less susceptible to bruising than those that fall on tarps or into nets when the tree is shaken with a stick or vibrated mechanically. Using large electric branch combs seems an intermediate solution—at least the olives do not crash to earth. Personally, I favor hand-picking, as I do for grapes.

One also needs to be concerned about how olives are stored. First, the time must be as short as possible between picking and milling so that no fermentation, which leads to unpleasant acidity in the oil, can take place. Two or three days storage seems to me a maximum. If olives are stored at 5 °C the period can be longer (up to forty-five days) without affecting product quality, but this requires large, and thus expensive, cold storage spaces that I have rarely seen on my travels.

Now to the milling itself. Everything and nothing has been said and written about this. According to the traditional image, pressing is carried out using a stone wheel turned by a couple of donkeys, with the olives crushed to a rough purée that is spread on round, flat basketwork *scourtins*. The *scourtins* are then slipped into a screw

Still splendid after years of faithful service, this antique olive oil pump graces Olivier & Co.'s counter on the Ile Saint-Louis in Paris. Such pumps have long been replaced by modern bottling machines, but Olivier & Co. still use this one from time to time (facing page).

press and squeezed, the oil running into large clay jars. It is transported in amphorae and then transferred into smaller vessels and bottles. I know of only a few mills producing oil in this ancestral way and even here the process has been modernized by the use of mashing hammers instead of millstones and hydraulic presses instead of screw presses.

Today, most olives sent through an electric crusher are reduced to a room-temperature paste which must be softened with a bit of warm water before it can be worked in a mill that continues to crush as it sways right to left squeezing out the oil. The oil runs out very slowly—the first product being, of course, the best—and takes only about twenty minutes per batch. The method is more modern and faster as well, but the oil remains olive "juice." The results are good—providing, of course, that at each step the imperatives of good quality are respected. This is what I look for and what Christophe verifies when we visit the mills.

On the subject of quality, when will we stop talking about "première pression à froid" (first cold press) in France? This, or some similar expression, without which a bottle of olive oil has little chance of selling, has been meaningless for many decades. It dates from the time when presses lacked the power to extract all the oil at a blow and it was necessary to do a second milling and pressing adding hot water, which naturally resulted in an inferior product. However, once powerful modern hydraulic presses were introduced, only a single pressing was necessary. We have made a pointless slogan of the problems of the old process.

I do not wish to enter into the debate about hydraulic presses and the continuous extraction system, but I will make one observation: modernity has much good in it when it involves rigorous hygiene.

In the final phase of production, the crude oil must be purified by removing the water and other impurities. Should it be decanted or centrifuged? That is the question. Decanting is done in big stainless steel tanks over a period of thirty to thirty-six hours, which is how long it takes for the oil

A traditional press used to crush the pile of scourtins *filled with olive paste (above).*
Plugged with cork and dressed in burlap, these 5-quart jugs were long used in Portugal
to preserve and transport olive oil (facing page).

to settle over the water. Centrifugation, a lot more brutal but also a lot quicker, is done in an electric centrifuge. Of course, purists prefer the good old decanting process, which requires, in addition to the thirty or so hours of settling, a further two months of slowly wringing out the sediment from the oil. Nowadays, however, the two-month period has been replaced by a method of filtering the oil through paper or an algae-based screen to remove any suspended particles that might mar its beautiful golden appearance.

Filtering takes place just prior to bottling. There is nothing obligatory about it, though, and some prefer their oil unfiltered, claiming it preserves the bouquet better. However, we have found that the unfiltered oils are not to everyone's taste and are sometimes more fragile than their filtered sisters.

It goes without saying that I pay careful attention to hygiene. Quaint dirtiness and the patina of age have nothing to do with good-quality olive oil—quite the contrary. Olive oil takes on the tastes of the things that come into contact with it. Dirt, like

These charmingly antiquated metal oil cruets (above)
with their long necks are ideal for pouring oil on vegetables, grilled fish or a piece of bread.
Bursting with their youthful bouquets of citrus and flowers, these new Andalusian oils
are still slightly cloudy (facing page).

chemical products, must be resolutely banned from production areas. In a mill, everything is water-washed. The oil must have as little contact with the air as possible. For extra virgin oil, production areas are regularly checked by the authorities. If it is found that they do not meet strict hygiene regulations, they lose their classification.

Finally, as with wine, quality involves limited production. On average, about 10 lbs. of olives are required to produce 1 quart of oil. However, for quality oils—those produced in the manner described above—the production ratio is reduced by about 10%. For the *mère goutte* (mother drop)—the oil obtained at the moment the olives are crushed and without pressing—it takes 25 lbs. of fruit for 1 quart of oil. Rare stuff indeed.

All the elements listed above come together to produce an olive *cru* in which we can find, as with wine, certain essential characteristics from year to year, even if the bouquets change according to whether it has been a hot or cold, wet or dry season.

If olive oil *crus* differ in some fundamental way from wine *crus*, it is in the growing and aging processes. Olive oil must be consumed young. No oxidation should take place. For this reason, I put the harvest date on my oils. That way, those who love olive oil can best profit from the youth, freshness and intensity of the bouquets, the pure taste and, of course, the distinctiveness of the different *crus*, which fade as the months go by.

TASTING OLIVE OIL

How should olive oil be tasted? How can we best appreciate its bouquet, its texture, its aftertaste? How do we assess its potential for combining well with the other elements of a dish, even if this is simply a salad?

*Bread, at the heart of the healthy Mediterranean diet,
is the favored companion of wine and olive oil. To taste and savor an olive oil,
nothing beats a simple piece of bread, soft in the center and crusty
on the outside (facing page). The bread from the bakery in Mane (above)
is perfect for tasting Provençal oils, as well as those from other oil-producing regions
such as Andalusia and Tuscany.*

Our in-house taster Eric Verdier begins with the bouquet. Pour a spoonful of oil into a small glass and warm the glass in your hand to free the scents. Inhale several times in succession, or do as they do in Corsica and dribble a few drops into the palm of your hand, warm it by stirring a bit with your finger and sniff.

Tasting gives you a wider range of choices. You can do it by the spoonful, calmly and sensually. Look carefully at the color of the oil as it is poured into the spoon. Inhale the bouquet before rolling it lightly in your mouth, as you would a wine. Keep your mouth firmly closed so that all the hints that make up a particular savor touch the palate: a glimmer of sweetness reminiscent of almond milk on the tip of the tongue, a prick of acidity that licks along the interior of the cheek, a touch of bitterness at the back when the oil slips down the throat leaving behind the aroma of fruits, flowers or leaves, an impression of fullness or of fluidity that make up a memory of an oil.

Using this first method you appreciate the texture of the oil. In the second one you benefit from the superb gesture of the gourmet, all too often forbidden by the rules of the table: oiling the bread. The very thought of dipping a piece of bread into this beautiful golden liquid lying in the saucer is a pleasure in itself. We know of adepts of both tasting methods. And all take care to rinse their mouths with water or white wine between two oils.

There is, however, a third tasting method, and it is the one I prefer. A potato, steamed and sliced, provides an excellent platform for olive oil. For refreshing your mouth afterward use a piece of apple, an idea suggested to me by some American friends.

More advanced, more complex and professional than the methods discussed above is testing the oils with different combinations of food. This can lead to a range of discoveries, the most obvious of which is that the same oil doesn't work for every sauce. Finding the right oil for a particular fish, a hot meat, a cold chicken, a very ripe tomato, a little snip of goat's cheese, a simple spaghetti or roast figs can be a very interesting game on an otherwise gloomy winter's evening. You don't need much to play, just two or three bottles of different *crus*, a few simple dishes and a couple of game gourmet players. No other rules are necessary and improvisation is encouraged. Pleasing surprises are guaranteed.

In the charming little village of Dauphin in Haute-Provence,
the baker prepares the traditional fougasse *bread with olive oil. Enjoy it on its own,*
with an apéritif or accompanied by a small salad, anchovies,
or fresh goat's milk cheese (facing page).

IT ALL BEGAN IN PROVENCE

Before starting out on my voyage of olive oil discovery, I carried out a highly symbolic ritual. More than forty years after my first visit at the side of my father, I returned to the Monessargues mill with my Oliviers & Co. colleagues, Laurent, Marie-Claire and Christophe.

Julien Masse, the *moulinier* I had met in my youth, was still operating his press, over eighty years old and with his memories of my father still intact. Julien is the soul of the "moulin de la cascade," as we call the Monessargues mill. Alerted to our presence by the barking of his dogs, he welcomed us with a good-humored mistrust in his eye, looking us up and down. His olive oil, the "good stuff," merits a little caution, no?

"You want to see the press?" He shoves open a sliding door and flings his arm toward the opening, "There it is." Julien is proud but seems a bit disillusioned, passing his knotty fingers over the place where a visor used to grace his cloth cap. The press hadn't moved an inch; it was exactly as I remembered it. His nephews now do most of the work. "Eat the oil and you'll live to be as old as an olive tree," says Julien. The oil still brings to mind his *fêtes royales*: three baked potatoes, a hard boiled egg, a few anchovies, a celery heart and a country salad. The simple memory of a slice of bread rubbed with garlic, topped with a bit of tomato and olive oil brings back his years as a day laborer in the fields. His face lights up.

In his strong voice Julien told us a few interesting anecdotes about his competitors. And then he had us taste a little of his own product, his own "waste oil" as he ironically calls it. One can see why: it is dark, thick and strong smelling, with a veil of bitterness and a bouquet of oak and thyme, pungent like the earth. It is a disturbing brew, which ruffles the palate and leaves no one neutral. In the country around some hate it, while others venerate it. There is no middle ground. The *huile de Lurs*, as Julien's oil

This lovely collection of old labels touts the virtues of Provençal oil
with a great deal of charm. In the foreground, a more recent example,
designed by the writer Peter Mayle for Oliviers & Co., asserts that "Olive oil is liquid sun"
and uses Mediterranean ochers to create warmth in a sparer modern style (above).
An artichoke seasoned with salt and pepper and enhanced with Corsican,
Istrian or Sicilian olive oil makes for a real delicacy (facing page).

is known locally, is one that provokes controversy, sometimes even hot words.

But we weren't there to judge the merits of these differing factions but to witness the end of an era. The end of an era of poetic pragmatism and do-it-yourself mores which gave everyone a chance to make his own world work for him. We were there to watch the concise gesture, the mute precision of hands moving rapidly over the grinding stones, seizing a handful of glistening olive paste. We were there to contemplate the nature of this dark liquid that runs out as green gold.

Once we had concluded our pilgrimage, I began voyaging, cautiously at first, with a reconnaissance mission in my own territory. Most of the hills in Haute-Provence harbor a rustic and rather untamable tree known as the *aglandau*. It produces fruit that has a slightly bumpy surface and whose color changes rapidly from green to purple just before the harvest in late October and early November. The Aglandau variety is found almost everywhere in the region, from Les Mées to Manosque. But it is impossible to find two oils that are similar.

Olive harvesting has traditionally been done by slipping a "comb"
through the branches and knocking the fruits down into nets spread under the trees,
as seen here in the Var region (above and facing page).
The olives are then carried to the mill in willow baskets.

Les Mées oil—the pure Aglandau so dear to André Pinatel, president of the Les Mées cooperative—is a lovely deep dark hue. It is strong and savory with a pronounced artichoke bouquet. The oil produced around Manosque is generally clearer than this, perhaps a bit less fiery and with an apple and green tomato bouquet. Of course, this description is not set in stone: the oils vary from season to season. Each "vintage" has its special quality, but unlike wine, it doesn't last; you can keep a *cru* for perhaps a year, maybe two, but after that it no longer satisfies the demanding palate. Olive oil is truly the pleasure of a season.

What accounts for the difference between the oils of Les Mées and Manosque? Is it the soil? Les Mées trees are planted on an alluvial plain, Manosque ones on the limestone of the hills. Is it microclimate? How different does the weather have to be? Is it pressing techniques? It is possible to think of many hypotheses and even scare up a debate on the physiology of the vegetable world, but the loveliest explanation I've heard is Joseph Ramero's. Joseph is a retired miller from the Les Mées cooperative. "If Les Mées oil is so different from the others, it's because trees planted in the plain of the Durance River get the last of the sun, the light of sundown," he explains.

Here in Haute-Provence, as elsewhere in the region, olives are harvested by hand or with combs that scrape through the branches, forcing them to fall into nets spread on the ground beneath. Harvesting is an anxious business and great care is taken to avoid bruising the olives since this can have a serious effect on the quality of the oil. Training in the necessity of care in harvesting has been carried out among olive growers in Haute-Provence. The right to bear the *Appellation d'Origine Contrôlée* (controlled appellation) is the grower's reward.

The Aglandau is not exclusive to Haute-Provence and in fact is grown throughout Provence, running from the Var to the Vallée des Baux, through the region of Aix, where it is sometimes called the Verdale, because the locals insist on the specialness of their region and want the olives to reflect that specialness, if only in name—as if identifying tree varieties wasn't difficult enough already!

What is there new to be said about the Vallée des Baux, a much publicized region that has done so much to raise the reputation of olive oil? The Verdale,

"Once picked," writes Michel Biehn in his Couleurs de Provence,
"the olives may wait a week before being taken to the mill, but not longer as that would affect the quality of the oil." The olives are carefully sorted to eliminate leaves, twigs and spoiled fruit, as here in Provence-Côte-d'Azur (facing page).

the Salonenque, the Grossane, the Picholine, among others, are becoming well known to olive lovers, especially as table olives. But this wonderfully rich agricultural region has recently been rewarded for its pains with an *Appellation d'Origine Contrôlée*, in addition to being the height of elegance. But, as everywhere, you've got to taste and taste again before making your choice.

It is always a pleasure for me to visit Henri Noaro, director of La Cravenco, at harvest time. The estate sits on the windy plain of the Crau River at the far end of the Vallée des Baux. Henri speaks of his trade with the talent and skill of a wine maker. Each year he pre-pares a series of new oil samples for our team to taste, giving us judicious advice on the origin and the quality of the lots of the olives selected. When it comes to the olive, Henri is informed like no one else.

The whole Cheylan family, and Christine in particular, is Henri Noaro's counterpart in the country around Aix. Christine has succeeded in a very short time in making Château Virant olive oil a *grand cru*, enabling us to choose between the freshly pressed *cuves* of Aglandau and Salonenque. Not far from La Fare les Oliviers and Aix, Château Virant is one of the last large estates with vast olive groves in the country around.

Moving toward the Var, the countryside changes, breaking up. The orchards become smaller. You must cross industrialized areas and towns and villages of seamless concrete. The farms are disappearing: the working groves are giving way to the olive tree as a landscaping feature in urban settings.

I am reminded of a very old olive miller, Eugène Mauro, whom I have not seen since my first voyage. Eugène ran one of the very last hand-operated presses in the center of Draguignan. We spent the morning together one day. There was a bond between him and his clients, who were as old as he was but who all addressed him with the formal *vous*. He was formal with me too, but, without seeming to pay me any attention, he told me his life story, as if he were talking to himself. There was much

Of the same family as the ash and lilac, the olive is a robust,
medium-sized tree (facing page). Its evergreen leaves, which are deep green on one side
and silver on the other, reflect the sun in a special way familiar to those who know
the Mediterranean region. Pierre Bergé, president of Yves Saint-Laurent,
is an ardent devotee of Provence and its olive oils, particularly his own, Mas Théo,
produced by Jean-Marie Cornille's traditional press at Maussane (above).

fatalism and regret in his words. It was the story of a world on the road to extinction, just like that of Julien Masse.

Eugène said, "Me, I come from the unlucky country, the country of fields of olive and goats." A massive man without any real fat about him, he no longer felt as lively as he once did. All the same, he took care to do his two daily pressings, sitting down on his bench from time to time to catch his breath.

One of Eugène's clients came up from Toulon. He told me he had lived in a countryside that today is overwhelmed by an all-encompassing urbanization: "All those olive trees were so lovely. So many that you might say they were like the sea. Now, they've planted some pines. But the gardens are so small, really small!"

Like the countryside, the olive varieties are diverse. Bouteillan, Cayet Roux, Belgentiéroise, Ribier, Aglandau, Picholine

The quintessential image of traditional Provence: olives climbing a stone terrace on a dry hillside (above).

and Grossane are but some among dozens of varieties. They are all more or less ancient and not always clearly identified.

The whole of the Haut-Var in particular is an immense reservoir of varieties, but the trees are unfortunately too few to enable growers to fully exploit the exceptional richness. Some growers have, all the same, made specialties, as has the Callas press northwest of Draguignan, operated by Serge and Nicole Bérenguier. They produce a pure Ribier olive oil unique to the region. It is very sweet with a light bouquet of cool, crisp olives.

Other growers, such as Pierre Carra of Domaine Jasson in the Var, between Hyères and Le Lavandou, have put together expert mixes of the different varieties. At his La Londe des Maures property some miles from the sea, Pierre has cleared the under-growth from the hills and planted Aglandau, Cayon, Bouteillan, Grossane and even

Carefully corked, shiny metal estagnons *provide protection from light and air, the natural enemies of olive oil (above).*

a Moroccan variety known as Dahbia (which has the bouquet of forest fruits, particularly strawberry). He uses the Dahbia with brio to add a final touch to his mixes. Pierre is one of the great artisans of the olive in the Massif des Maures region.

In the Massif d'Estérel near Nice I was able to see another form of artisanal expertise, this time in logistics. The Cailletier olive trees grown between Grasse and Menton can reach a height of 30 feet, producing the little black olives we know as Olives de Nice. The Cailletier is an olive that has always been harvested late, at full maturity, in January or February. So, for the moment, the oil produced most often in the region is sweet, with a hazelnut and almond bouquet. Traditions have begun changing, though, and many growers are now trying to harvest in December to get an oil with more bite.

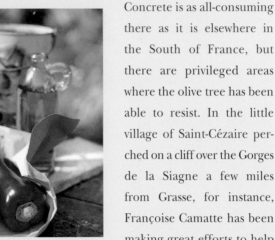

Because the Estérel's trees are so tall, so angular and so often grown in terraces marching high, harvesting requires serious thought. First, nets have to be laid out under the trees. The olives are then shaken from the branches by banging with a pole. Milling must follow on as soon as possible to avoid oxidation, but this isn't easy, as anyone who has driven along the winding roads of the back country in Provence will understand.

Over time I've formed a number of important friendships in the Nice region. Concrete is as all-consuming there as it is elsewhere in the South of France, but there are privileged areas where the olive tree has been able to resist. In the little village of Saint-Cézaire perched on a cliff over the Gorges de la Siagne a few miles from Grasse, for instance, Françoise Camatte has been making great efforts to help fellow growers improve quality and keep the olive competitive. Unfortunately, despite producing an excellent oil, Françoise does not have enough trees to make a marketable product. The Ranguin estate at Mougins has a similar problem, with very few olives for making oil, most of them going for olive paste production. Ranguin oil is, all the same, very fine indeed, with its milky aspect and bouquet of hawthorn and acacia honey.

As a companion to fresh peppers nothing beats a thick, silky Peloponnese
or fruity Haute-Provence olive oil (above). All olive varieties can be used to make oil
or consumed as table olives. Some, such as the Picholine or Lucques varieties,
lend themselves better than others to oil (facing page).
These Picholine olives coated in olive oil are ready for the apéritif.

Huile d'Olive
Piment
Aux Arômes Naturels
Concentrés
50 ml e
OLIVIERS & CO. - 04700 MANE - FRANCE

I have had success serving it with a grilled bass. For Ranguin, as for the groves at Saint-Cézaire, the problem remains agriculture's unequal struggle with real estate.

A bit further up country, not far from Contes, the village of Blausasc, planted on a rock, still uses techniques that belong more to a historical re-enactment in a museum than a modern business. This remarkable oil mill is worth describing, for it typifies the meticulous approach of the people in the region.

Built in the sixteenth century, the Blausasc mill works on the old Genoese principle of crushing the fruit with a stone wheel in a basinlike receptacle. Once the olive has been turned into paste, water is added to the basin and decanting takes place, the oil being scooped from the surface with a platelike spoon called a *feuille* (leaf). It is then poured into barrels. This is not a very productive method, for sure, and demands a great deal of patience. Moreover, it produces a light, and lightly aromatic, oil of very mediocre quality. Even the owner admits the mill is not a very profitable undertaking.

But then it's the atmosphere that pays at Blausasc. For a very small quantity of olives many elderly people are busily at work. They speak little and in dialect. It is as if all this was being done simply to preserve a tradition that is in danger of disappearing.

Ten miles or so farther up the road, the scene changes radically. One could almost be in Tuscany. The magnificent Château du Vignal sits discreetly on the flank of a hill crowned with neat terraces of olive. Henriette and Pierre Chiesa-Gautier-Vignal have spent many years putting this family property in order.

During the December harvest every-one here is busy producing the château's clear sun-colored olive oil, which has a rare sweetness and a strong almond and hazelnut bouquet. Like good wine makers (Henriette and Pierre have a vineyard near Lausanne as well as these groves), they follow their product through from start to finish. The cellar is a model of sparkling cleanliness and moderated temperature.

Discovering the Château du Vignal grounds with Henriette and Pierre was a very pleasant experience. Many springs dot the land and every tree receives a bit of water fresh from the earth. The hill is in the shape of a natural amphitheater with the trees as the happy spectators. The château has undergone a veritable Renaissance and is an example to be followed in other parts of the region.

A process perfected in sixteenth-century Florence allows us
to flavor olive oil with fresh plants. Spiced oil is exquisite over a plate of al dente *spaghetti,*
but it can be even better with a pinch of garlic or a few slices of grilled mullet.

This is in fact the case in the Ardèche region. In the foothills of the Cévennes, the northern limit of olive culture and therefore, according to historian Fernand Braudel, the limit of the Mediterranean world, olive-growing is effervescent. However, a lot remains to be done before the Ardèche can fully revive its heritage of olive cultivation, because it has been neglected for many years. But growers have started to replant the Rougette, a variety specific to the region which is producing a very promising oil. And the efforts in the Ardèche are an example that can be followed throughout the Languedoc, which has traditionally produced mostly table olives such as the Lucques from the Aude country.

Nyons and its environs are a region apart, halfway between Provence and the first Alpine peaks. Olive trees share the fields with vines and apricot orchards under the high protection of Mont Ventoux. The local Tanche variety is picked black and used both for oil and as a table olive. The oil is sweet and milky with a fairly pronounced hazelnut perfume. It is often of exceptional quality.

I have a good reason for keeping Nyons and the Nyons area for last, for in truth the real example for olive growers to follow is here. It was here that the *Appellation d'Origine Contrôlée* for olive oil was first introduced. It was also here that the rigorous guidelines that allow growers to benefit from its protection were laid down and strictly applied. As a result, gaining the *Appellation d'Origine Contrôlée* is an encouraging sign for olive production and a guarantee for the future. The continuing respect growers and mills show for the guidelines can only strengthen the excellent image of the whole region and, especially, that of the Nyons cooperative, whose work is already above reproach.

Corsica

Olives
Sabina, winter harvest.

Tasting notes
Nose of green grass and leguminous plants. Powerful flavor developing into a fine bitterness.

Suggestions for use
Spicy dishes, couscous, tajines, vegetable purées.

CORSICA: TWO HARVESTS A YEAR

I had to go to Balagne in the region of Calvi to be initiated into the Corsican method of determining an oil's good and bad points. You pour a few drops in the palm

All Mediterranean countries produce olive oils. These vary in strength, greenness, fruitiness and general sweetness or sharpness, with aromas ranging from the vegetal to the animal, smells of fruit, flowers and leaves, hints of bitterness and peppery undertones. As for wine, every olive oil cru *has its own distinctive personality (right, oils from Latium, Provence, Sicily, Istria and Sardinia).*

of the hand, stir with the finger and inhale. The heat generated by stirring brings out the bouquet. It is a remarkably effective method for detecting major problems such as rancidness or mildew (a wet hay smell), or a winey or burnt flavor—the kinds of faults that usually indicate technical problems in production or the use of poor-quality olives.

On the Ile de Beauté, because of the problems of harvesting in olive groves which are very inaccessible in bad weather, tradition dictates that oil is made in the spring with ripe olives that have fallen from the trees into nets. The resulting oil is of incomparable sweetness, with a very light *maquis* bouquet, but it is difficult to keep. This is often the case for late-harvested fruits, because they tend to oxidize rapidly. Today, because of the partial mechanization of harvesting techniques, some growers, especially those in the Balagne cooperative, are able to harvest in winter and are getting a strong oil with more fruit and aroma.

In Corsica, the olive is everywhere. On the heights of Niebbu, a narrow and isolated piece of country between the Agriates desert and Cap Corse, multi-century trees continue patient lives. Further south, in the Vallée de l'Ostricone, a nearly abandoned estate is undergoing a renaissance through the efforts of the owner's grandson. His aim is to make a quality oil with the local Sabina variety and we are going to try and help him.

At the Cagnano mill to the north of Bastia I experienced one of the most moving episodes of my voyage. There, in the mountains of Cap Corse, the winding road is lined with petrified trees, witnesses to the recent fires. But you still see exuberant, defiant olive trees that still closely resemble the ancestral oleaster.

One of the oldest mills in Corsica (now almost a museum) dates from the sixteenth century. Hidden under a grove of oak and cork trees in the heart of an abandoned hamlet on the sea's edge, it has the particularity of serving both as an olive and chestnut press. There is even a still, for a long time a secret part of operations. At this mill, olive oil production does not follow the usual procedure because, after harvesting, the olives are spread in an attic, where they are raked from time to time to keep them aired and thoroughly dried, like ham. Once dry they are ground and pressed. The oil produced is extremely strong, acrid and earthy—an "olive extract." This type of oil does not appeal to the contemporary palate and it's value is historical.

PORTUGAL: LOOKING FOR QUALITY

After France, where olive oil production is among the lowest in the Mediterranean basin, the transition to countries where olive growing makes up an important part of the local economy is striking.

Since the creation of the controlled appellation scheme and its application throughout Europe, Portuguese growers have made some progress toward meeting its standards but oil quality remains variable, due in particular to the olive fly, which causes enormous damage in plantations.

However, although quality is uneven, the Portuguese should be praised for their determination. Scorching drought and a gradual abandonment of the groves has contributed to an impression of poverty in all producing regions. This is the case at the Quinta de l'Alentejo, in the south of the country, which houses a family-run museum. The centerpiece is a huge wooden mill weighing many tons. The owner of the mill, aged ninety, lives in Estoril, the fashionable part of Lisbon. He, it seems, is entirely uninterested in what happens to his groves. The manager, a certain Senhor Leonardo, asked me to speak about France. He had lived there in his youth. As I spoke his eyes filled with tears. He had me taste his oil, which was, unfortunately, very acid. But the man was so kind and moving,

I found it impossible to tell him so. I just hadn't the heart.

Quinta de l'Alentejo is representative of the country as a whole, even though Portugal has embarked on a veritable race for quality. During a stop in the Trás-Os-Montes region in the northwest of the country, I heard a particularly amusing and revealing remark concerning the so-called "organic" classification of certain oils. Many producers, it was said, make organic oil, the reason being that they cannot afford pesticides and artificial fertilizers. This piece of irony says much about the situation in Portugal.

SPAIN: A LITTLE-KNOWN PALETTE OF OILS

Although production in Spain has dropped in recent years, largely because of drought in Andalusia, the country has been the world's biggest olive producer for two seasons past. Spanish oils are very diverse. Indeed, they are becoming ever more diverse both from one region or province to another and even within provinces and regions. For me, Spain was a whole new voyage of discovery.

Rainha Santa oil (facing page), the product of an organic grove
in Alentejo province in eastern Portugal, uses the Galaga variety.
Its grassy, citrus bouquet makes it ideal for raw or cooked green vegetables and grilled fish.
The Pons family of Lerida in Catalonia uses the Arbequina variety to produce
an extra virgin oil that is sweet, elegant and delicately fruity,
to be savored fresh over hot grilled fish or cold poultry (above).

It all began, of course, in Catalonia, a province that abounds in olive trees and which has succeeded in producing two controlled appellation oils. Around Lerida, southwest of Barcelona, the almond trees share the reddish earth with the olive. Here was born the Arbequina, the little olive typical of the region. It produces a very sweet oil, with animal undertones and a milky, delicate almond bouquet, which goes well with fish, meat and cheese. It is hard to imagine Catalan cuisine without the subtle flavors and creamy texture of the Arbequina oils. Yet, the olive's history in the country is not so rosy as you might expect from this. According to legend, in the eighteenth century the Duke of Arbeca brought back from Greece a variety of olives and promised bonuses to those who succeeded in growing them. The whole region of Les Garrigues, south of Lerida, was immediately covered with the duke's olive trees. However, nobody saw a penny of the promised bonuses. Worse, when after years of rather frustrating patience the time came to harvest the olives for the first time, the duke, who had a complete monopoly on the mills, levied a tax on the oils produced and so wound up with a large part of the production. Since this time the millers say "olive oil is as good as gold."

In the region of Tarragona, to the south of Barcelona, lies the territory of Catalonia's second appellation, Surana, also a product of the Arbequina variety. However it's taste is quite distinct. It is sweeter and lacks the aromas of almond and toast. Might this be because of the influence of the nearby sea?

In Castille, in the vast groves of La Mancha, at the foot of the Toledan hills, the leading olive variety is the Cornicabra. Its oil has a taste that brings together, rather oddly, a kind of fruity sweetness and a strong bitterness. It is so strong, in fact, that I had a coughing fit after having eaten a few crumbs of bread soaked in it, much to the amusement of the miller who had invited me into his kitchen for the tasting.

Is it possible that olive-growing was born somewhere in one of these white villages, on the slopes of these arid mountains?

Spain is one of the greatest producers of olive oil.
These olive groves are in Jaen province (facing page). At Baena in Andalusia,
the best of tradition allied to high-performance modern techniques enables
the Nunez de Prado family to produce dense, fruity, exemplary oils which marry superbly
with Andalusian cuisine (above).

It is easy to believe it when you arrive in the Sierra Magina, in western Andalusia. On the heights of this mountain-ous massif, which has its own microclimate, the men and women of the Jimena cooperative produce, using the Picual variety, one of the most delicious oils in the region, a fruit full of character and quite bitter.

Young and energetic, the Jimena cooperative's managers struggle gamely to achieve the highest quality and they welcomed me with open arms. As I was leaving, an eighty-year-old grower, who had kept to himself till then, caught me by the arm and said, "If you want a good oil, don't go looking for it with your eyes. Use your nose. If you smell the slightest unpleasant odor when you set foot inside a mill, turn around and walk out." It's a piece of advice I always follow and which has helped me a great deal.

In the Sierra Subbetica region of Andalusia, near Cordoba, the Baena cooperative produces a delightful oil made from the Picudo variety. It is a subtle product, fruity, sun-yellow, with a bouquet of lemon peel and blackcurrant buds, and a slightly sugary flavor.

The controlled appellation for Baena oil includes a few villages that produce as much oil as the whole of Provence. My visit there held many surprises. The industrial plant was immense and the vast storage facilities contained numerous immaculately clean vats of oils which were classified by flavor. I tasted dozens of oils before choosing a few samples to bring back to Manes and the rest of my team. It was a gourmet's game I could play a hundred times again.

Baena may have easily been my final resting place, but I had other regions to visit

Born on the fertile hills of Tuscany in a very mild microclimate,
Del Ponte oil (above, left) has a fruity savor with a grassy hint which makes it especially good
with salads and vegetables. Calogiuri oil (right) from Lizzanello in Puglia,
is a lacrima di affiorimento, *the king of oils, neither centrifuged nor filtered*
and produced in tiny quantities. Aaromatic and sweet, the oil is delicious.

and provinces other than Andalusia to inspect. It is always a pleasure to visit Andalusia, for there is much that can be learnt from the way they marry pleasure and refinement, food and aesthetics there. Everything is done with brio and finesse. With its fried foods and its mayonnaise, its tortillas and salads, its seafood and croquettes, its gazpacho and *salmorejo*, the cooking of Andalusia is proof of the culinary genius that lies within the olive.

TUSCANY: LOVELIEST OF ALL

If there is one place that symbolizes the Mediterranean art of living it is incontestably Italy. The colors and the perfumes, the houses and objects, the cooking and the music—all come together in an ambiance very much resembling happiness. Even when everything is going wrong, there's always a warm plate of spaghetti or a little corner of blue in the somber sky to cheer you.

Is this a clichéd image? Maybe. All the same, traveling up and down the country in search of lost oils is far from what you might call punishment. Every region of Italy has its mythical town, a sacred place. Jewels of tiny villages and glimpses of idyllic landscapes studded my voyage through Italy with magic moments.

Tuscany, which contributes only 3% of the oil produced in Italy, has the enviable reputation of making some of the country's finest oils. That is a testament to the exceptional work accomplished by its growers and producers.

My personal Tuscany begins at Lucca, although for administrative purposes it begins well before then. It is from the hills of Lucca that you are first able to see the great farms: Castello, Fattoria, Azienda, Podere, Tennuta, Villa. All are magnificent and, for the most part, dedicated to the grape and the olive. Crossing Tuscany is a delight. The countryside is a harmonious series of hills and valleys embroidered green and silver and spiked with cypresses and incredibly well-preserved villages. It is a luminous country with a shade of melancholy, sufficiently cold in winter and sufficiently sunny in summer to make you live in what seems a perfect equilibrium.

Tuscany currently produces a strong, distinctive oil made up of four varieties. The Frantoio is the largest contributor, followed by the Moraiolo, Leccino and Pendolino. The oils are fruity, strong and peppery, with an artichoke bouquet. This is oil that is marvelous in a tomato salad with a few slices of Mozzarella and a few leaves of basil. Obviously it does the business for pasta too and, generally, for all vegetables.

But the region is not uniform and has several distinct areas: Colle Luchese, Colle Fiorentini, Colle Sense, Chianti Classico and Chianti Rufina. The uninitiated have difficulty seeing the differences because Tuscany seems so much of a piece. But the nuances, even the slight ones, reveal themselves well enough when it comes to the aromas, colors and densities of olive oils. Certain among them have a smoothness of texture that covers the palate in sweetness before revealing an unsuspected strength of taste. Others are fresher, more mineral, with a touch of liqueur. What is clear is that the Tuscans have made a science of olive oil, combined with incomparable commercial know-how. Unfortunately, there isn't space here to detail my many meetings and chance encounters in the region. I have been received by ancient families, marquis and counts, and by the simplest country folk. In every case the welcome has always been admirable.

The elegant gesture seems to be part of life in Tuscany. The Gratis typify my experiences. The family lives in Chianti Rufina, on the northern limit of the Tuscan olive-growing region. They welcomed me with open arms, grilling slices of bread in the fireplace. Sprinkled with oil just a few hours off the press and a few grains of salt and washed down with a glass of household Chianti, they transformed the sharp cold of a winter's day into a lovely memory.

UMBRIA: SWEETNESS OF LIGHT, SWEETNESS OF OILS

The contentment that travels with you on a voyage in Italy during the November-December harvest season is reflected in the light, especially in Umbria. In winter it has a unique

quality that lends the gentle countryside around Assisi a particular charm.

Toward the end of the day, an orange-pink light bathes the Umbrian hills in a poignant, profound melancholy. One evening in particular comes to mind. I had spent the day tasting oils at the mills with the mayor of a little village called Giano dell'Umbria. Pointing up to a hill behind the village he showed me the Abbey of San Felice, which has given its name to one of the local varieties of olive. He waited till night fell at about 10 p.m. before taking me up to see the place. Don Giulio, a missionary, was waiting for us when we arrived and showed us around. He told me the history of the region and taught me about the role played by the San Felice monks in the development of olive-growing there. The patience and extreme care shown to me by both the mayor and the missionary paralleled their sense of how the olive should be treated, a sense transmitted over centuries. I tasted many oils, one of which particularly attracted my attention. It was sharp, with a perfume of cashew, almond and milk.

Some of Italy's finest: the fruity and ample Tenuta de Corato from Puglia,
made from the Coratina variety; an elegant thoroughbred Tuscan oil from the San Guido estate;
and strong and grassy Sardinian oil, Argiolas Iolao.
Each oil is extra virgin, of course (above).

LIGURIA: AN ALMOST LEGENDARY OIL

In the north, Liguria, close to the border with France, has some of the most celebrated olive oils. When you arrive at the town of Imperia, the most striking thing is the smell of olives, or more exactly olive paste, which is very strong everywhere. I suppose this should not be surprising, since Imperia is home to a good many olive-based enterprises and has been for better than one hundred years.

A trip to the museum of the olive run by the Carli company is *de rigueur* before any meeting with local producers. In Liguria, the olive-growing methods are similar to those used around Nice. Indeed, the trees are almost the same. The only thing that really separates the regions is the border. The oils produced from the local Taggiasca variety have a reputation for refinement, sweetness and fruitiness, but it is difficult to find an oil that combines all three qualities. It was hard work tasting olive oil in Liguria. I had to climb up to Luciasco, a little village perched up above the Oneglia valley. The craggy slopes of the mountains are covered with tall olive trees planted in well-maintained terraces.

Dino Abbo has been working in his mill on the ground floor of his home for many years with the sole aim of creating quality. Every evening he takes apart, cleans and reassembles his press. Every evening he scrupulously scrubs out the *scourtins*. A lovely odor of oil wafts up from the cellars

Latium

Olives
Frantoio.

Tasting notes
Nose of superb finesse and intensity. In the mouth it is rich with a beautiful development of flavors. A harsh, mineral, deep oil.

Suggestions for use
Pasta, tomatoes, fresh Brousse cheese.

where he keeps his vats: this is sufficiently rare to be noted. His grinding stones are fixed in such a way that they do not crush the olive pits along with the flesh —a way of avoiding any bitterness in the oil.

Not far from Lucinasco, the Gandolfo brothers have built a brand new press on the side of a mountain. Their whole production is certified organic under European law and their oil, which I tasted along with a glass of the regional white wine, is astonishingly good. I watched them sort out the olives before they went into the press: they never hesitated to reject handfuls, saying "That's the price of quality." I believe them.

DAZZLED AMONG THE SABINES

I owe my encounter with Sabine oil to Roman friends of mine, Lydia and Paolo Colonelli. They organize a contest to determine the best olive oils made by small producers, many of whom also had professions in Rome. They meet regularly and vote for a winner: that day it was a musician. None of the oils from among these urban producers really fascinated me, however. My hostess noticed my disappointment and next morning she took me off to the Masciocchi groves in the Sabine hills, about 30 miles from Rome. The Masciocchi family, from grandmother to grandchildren, welcomed us with delicious *bruschettes* (lightly grilled toast sprinkled with oil). The difference between the oils I had tasted the night before was truly a difference between day and night. But the family operation is small and the production, based on Frantoio olives, is no more than 1,500 gallons per year. It is an oil as precious as a jewel metaphorically and literally. After a visit to the groves and the mill, the family took me to the terrace. We could see the dome of St. Peter's in the distance. "How could we live elsewhere than here?" one of the brothers said.

SOUTHERN ITALY: ARID CHARM

Olive production in the Puglia plain, around the secretive and disconcerting city of Bari, is an institution. The harvest begins with table olives in early autumn. These are enormous, the size of plums, and are eaten in the evening with the family or while chatting with friends in the streets. Sold in cornets like French fried potatoes, they are a fixture of the *passeggiata*, the evening promenade so often interrupted by the exchanging of family news between friends and neighbors.

The oil olive harvest begins in early winter and lasts into February. The farms, with their exquisite architecture, are surprisingly beautiful. The vast, rocky arid spaces, the dry earth that is slightly salty, the sea air and summer sun all work to produce a characteristic bouquet of hay and fruit that marries so well with vegetables such as artichokes, beans and celery.

Going up the Adriatic coast to Abruzzi, I arrived in the "green triangle" around Loretto Aprutino, not far from Pescara. Here there is an impressive concentration of trees on a small strip of country protected from the cold on one side by the Apennines and on the other by the Adriatic. Olives ripen early here, with the harvest starting in October and ending in December. The oil is sweet, very green and with an apple and almond bouquet.

SARDINIA AND SICILY: THE MAGIC ISLES

Sardinia and Sicily belong to the same cult of olive oil and both islands are covered in groves. In northern Sardinia, the mountain sides are encircled by stout low walls of fat stones which contain very old olive trees. The groves are enclosed by fences, a rare sight in the Mediterranean region. At the heart of this dry countryside, the circular plateau of Giara di Gesturi and the surrounding valleys seem astonishingly green and fertile. Sheep can be seen grazing among the trees. From time to time one catches a glimpse of one of the little wild horses that flee at the sight of a human being.

Shown here in elegant bottles, decanted (left)
and undecanted (right) oils are easily distinguished.

This charmingly wild country produces an oil in its image: a light touch of bitterness on a background of mouth-filling fruity sweetness. The oil gets its savor from the Tonda. This is the standard variety in Sardinia and it gives off a strong apple odor when cut. It brings to mind the simple meals eaten by shepherds—bread, a slice of Pecorino, a country salad.

The producer of the particular oil I tasted, Signor Pirisi, a professor of agricultural toxicology at the University of Cagliari, is himself a product of the old Sardinia nobility. Around a café table, some of the neighbors were surprised that a Frenchman would come so far to taste the local wares. Signor Pirisi took me into the groves and showed me how to recognize the perfect degree of maturity of each of the different varieties of olive without relying solely on color. With a knife, he cut the olives in two and showed me that the flesh contained very little oil in spite of its mature-looking color. In a small popular restaurant in Cagliari's old town, we had a lovely meal of sliced Poutargue cheese in olive oil, spaghetti in grated Poutargue—with olive oil, of course—and grilled mullet.

In Sicily I was often disappointed by the production of the cooperatives but impressed by some treasures hidden away on private farms. At Menfi in the Belice valley on the south coast, for instance, where olives grow among orange and lemon trees and vines cling onto slopes that slip right into the sea, lies the La Gurra property. Owned by an ancient Sicilian noble family and run by descendant Nicolo Ravidà from his home at Palazzo Ravidà, the property produces an oil that is a subtle combination of the Biancolilla, Cerasuola and the Nocellara del Belice olive varieties.

The Biancolilla is responsible for the soft texture and green color, the Cerasuola for the perfumes and the Nocellara del Belice for its structure, exactly as might be the case for a wine blend. After the instructive tasting in my host's *palazzo*, we went to the estate's broad expanse of groves, from which both the sea and the small city of Menfi may be seen. The streets of Menfi were covered in the dust carried by the sirocco.

On the Ravidà estate everything was done to obtain optimum quality. After each day's harvest the olives are brought to the mill, perfuming the night with the scent of fresh oil. There is no waiting, no fermentation and no mixing. This care enables Ravidà to produce an oil of exceptional quality. Before milling begins in earnest, some table olives are sacrificed in a maiden run that serves to clean the machinery; the oil obtained is used for cooking in the family kitchens. There was a final moment of bliss at Palazzo Ravidà: a cool glass of La Gurra's white wine on a terrace overlooking the sea.

In Italy I learned to understand the primary importance of the soil for superior *crus* produced in optimum conditions using the most modern growing and pressing techniques.

GREECE: DIFFERENT ISLES, DIFFERENT *CRUS*

In Greece I was to discover a world more rooted in the past than any other of the countries I had visited, even as it adapts rapidly to the contemporary world and its expectations of quality.

Under the blue sky that arches over the thousands of olive trees of the Peloponnese, Thessaly and Crete and the isles that dot the Aegean Sea, the varieties of olive available are innumerable. With twenty-two controlled appellations and protected origin registrations, Greece beats all the records among the Mediterranean olive growers—and also causes not a little confusion for those in pursuit of olive truths. I cannot name all the *crus* and in any case I haven't tasted them all —that will require many more voyages.

It was in the Peloponnese, after crossing the mountains of Arcadia and going down into Kalamata and the Gulf of Messenia, that I found one of the most accomplished Greek oils. In the remote area of Mani, the peaceable valleys are filled with seas of shivering olive trees interrupted by towerlike, gray and white stone villages. People are proud and protect-ive here, and electricity has been very slow to penetrate. Life revolves around the olive.

From the earliest days of November whole families go into the fields to lay canvas tarps under the trees before beginning the hard work of knocking the branches with poles until the olives fall. The olives, called Koroneiki, fall onto the tarps before being placed in airy canvas sacks—nylon and plastic are strictly prohibited— and placed at the side of the road for pick up by the farm cooperative trucks. A few yards from the sea, where the temperature is less fierce, the olives are washed, sorted and milled before being filtered slowly through, first, balls of raw cotton and then fine-weave paper.

After visiting the operations, I talked things over with Mani's current cooperative manager and his father, the founder of the establishment. We sat in the family café, on the terrace, overlooking the sea. The ambiance

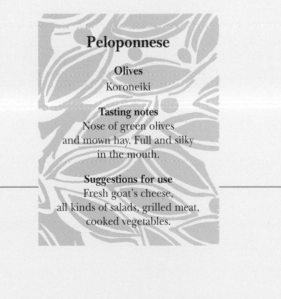

Peloponnese

Olives
Koroneiki

Tasting notes
Nose of green olives
and mown hay. Full and silky
in the mouth.

Suggestions for use
Fresh goat's cheese,
all kinds of salads, grilled meat,
cooked vegetables.

was very relaxed and open. The father was extremely happy to be selling the country's oil in France. He had been traveling the highways and byways of the Mediterranean region for forty years to learn the newest techniques and keep up with changes. He had had a lot of trouble convincing the inhabitants of his village of the real necessity of progress both in cultivation and care of the trees and in oil production. This was why, he said, my visit made him so happy. He thought that his work had not been in vain. Foreigners now thought it worth their while to make the trip to buy his oil.

I found conditions similar to those in Mani in central Chalcedon, the peninsula of northern Greece where Mount Athos and its celebrated monasteries lie. At the farm of Gerakini, I discovered an exquisite oil, intense and peppery, made from the Karydolia and Prassinolia varieties. These are harvested very early and of course hand-picked. The table olive was the tradition in Chalcedon and it has not been easy to turn to production of a *grand cru* oil. But what a success it is!

It was a long search from the Aegean to the Ionian seas by way of Crete to find an island oil. At Lesbos, also known as Mytilini, an island off the coast of Turkey (and where its influence can be strongly felt),

there are still many olive trees. The foot of each tree is hemmed by a little stone wall patiently built by men, but which blends in so well with the natural landscape. On the coasts are ruins of ancient presses, typically Turkish in design, with brick walls and large cylindrical chimneys. However Lesbos, with its air of an English Riviera resort where the clock stopped some time during the British Empire, seems more taken with tourism than with olive-growing.

On Cephalonia, the wise island of the Ionian Sea which protects little Ithaca with its mountains, the situation was more cheering. Along with honey and white wine, the island pools the cultivation of its old, brushy olive trees. The harvesting and milling of the Doppia olive are done communally. Even if the oil is not yet excellent, it shows great promise. The president of the local chamber of commerce took care to show me around, introducing me as his "French friend" and showering me with gifts. He made me promise to return once the cooperative had made the efforts necessary to bring the oil up to scratch. To recover from all these effusions and emotions I sat down in a restaurant and dug into a cooked lettuce well soaked in olive oil and copiously peppered. Reinvigorating.

Galilee, Provence, Andalusia, the Peloponnese, Tuscany…
these small flasks contain only small amounts
and are ideal for learning to taste olive oil (facing page).

CRETE: OILS TO DISCOVER

In the west of Crete, in the Bay of Kissamos, is the greatest grove on the isle, just a stone's throw from Khania, the celebrated tourist destination. The classic Koroneiki and the typical Tsounati are cultivated here in a microclimate on a rocky soil. The oil is fruity, delicate and very harmonious.

Further along, in the heights above the ancient capital of Knossos, are an abundance of olive trees laid out at regular intervals. These produce a little violet-colored fruit called Psiloelia (literally, "little olive") and look like those to be seen in certain areas of Corsica.

The olive tree is a great traveler. The fruit has long been one of Crete's major resources. In the palace of Minos, archeologists have brought to light jars capable of holding up to 2 tons of oil. They were found in rooms that were guarded day and night like treasure houses.

The oil of the Psiloelia gives a lovely sweet sensation in the mouth, but to me it lacks personality. Crete is one of the Greek islands I have the intention of exploring intensively in coming years. It would seem to hide many treasures that are easier to get at, perhaps, than those to be found in emerging areas such as Croatia.

CROATIA: GREEN GOLD IN A COUNTRY LOOKING FOR A RENAISSANCE

Istria, a peninsula jutting into the Gulf of Venice, presents many contrasts. Situated only a few miles from Trieste, its touristy coastline contrasts oddly with a back country that is quite poor and run down, although it has been spared the ravages of war. In such an atmosphere the Agrolaguna farm comes as little surprise, with its 1930s-style building complete with outmoded "Soviet realist" decor (which has disfigured so much of this part of the world). The vast offices, with their heavy wooden doors, are filled with old-fashioned furniture; there are no curtains and the paint is peeling. However, the very grimness of the scene makes the warmth of the people all the more striking. These olive-growing Croats blithely remind you that Istria is not Slav but rather Latin.

In the fields outside the Agrolaguna administrative building the carefully arranged trees are cared for by the Zuzic brothers. They run the farm with advice from the Trieste agronomic institute. The trees extend toward the horizon in fields which overlook the sea and . . . a nudist camp. Hidden in an old building in a village further inland, the ultra-modern press comes as a bit of a surprise, but you quickly succomb to the aroma of freshly pressed olives in the air.

I was fascinated by the intense and deep emerald green of the oil produced here. It is a superb product—dense, aromatic and strong, with a bouquet of artichoke and, of all things, chocolate. This is an oil

Istria

Olives
Lecino, Buga.

Tasting notes
Complex nose combining heart of artichoke, straw and dark chocolate. It has a fine bitterness giving it perfect balance.

Suggestions for use
Heart of artichoke, *filet mignon.*

you won't find on the grilled fish in the local restaurant, because it is too expensive for the locals. The quantities produced are excessively small and we cannot be sure of getting an adequate supply.

It must be said that the economic structure of olive-growing in the former Eastern bloc countries is still in flux and it will be some years before a clear picture emerges.

ISRAEL:
CULTURAL CRADLE
OF OLIVE OIL

In northern Galilee, as you reach the Lebanese border, the road passes through immense groves containing thousands of trees. The road links two culturally important villages: 'Akko, the biblical name of St.-Jean-d'Acre, and Zefat, the mythical town of the Kabbala where today many artists and intellectuals have settled.

A major part of the oil produced in Israel comes from olives grown in Galilee, even if the rest of the region also has its groves. Many olives also arrive from the other side of the border, because a number of Lebanese growers readily sell their harvests to Israeli mills, which offer

better prices than they can get in Lebanon.

Dr. Eger, an Israeli agronomist, selects the best olives from this zone without giving much thought to frontiers or politics. He is an exceptional man, charming, warm and generous. His parents managed to escape the Holocaust and, on reaching the Promised Land, they set up in the Jezreel Valley at the foot of Mount Carmel. It is a special region that has traditionally served as a commercial link between the coastal and mountain-dwelling peoples.

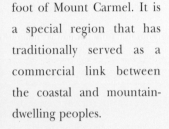

About twenty years ago Dr. Eger had to make a radical change of life because of a serious heart problem due to a dangerously high cholesterol level. His physician told him to eat more olive oil, so he decided to quit his old job and go to work looking after what he calls his "medicine." His oils are made from the four major olive varieties found in Israel: Souri, Barnea —the two dominant fruits—and Nabali and Manzanillo. Common all over the Middle East, including Lebanon, the Souri produces a green, peppery oil, fiery and grassy with a light honey taste. The Barnea gives a sweeter oil with a lightly fruity taste

This immense chandelier in the Oliviers & Co. shop on the rue de Buci in Paris is made from olive oil taster flasks and was designed by Colette Neyrard (above).

and a bouquet of mown hay, golden apples and jujube. In Israel it is difficult to find mixes of different oils because tradition prefers single variety products. There is another local particularity: in restaurants olive oil is never accompanied by a bottle of vinegar, but rather of lemon juice.

Heading in the direction of Lake Tiberias, in the east, I met a mill operator who, while at first seeming quite dour, finally showed himself to be rather pleasant and welcoming. Once a professional soldier, he had developed a passion for olives and decided to go into business. He went to Italy and bought modern equipment and set up his mill in the mountains about 10 miles from Nazareth. I had hardly arrived at his house when, as he talked with me, he cooked up a little mezze —Middle Eastern appetizers—including hummus (purée of chickpeas and olive oil) and homemade bread. This oil tasting was sheer delight.

Later, following advice given by my host, I went to a kibbutz in lower Galilee specializing in organic produce, kosher milk, butter, dry vegetables and olive oil. I am dying to introduce this oil made from the Souri variety to some of my ecology-minded American friends.

TUNISIA: OILS TO DISCOVER

Invited to dinner by a family with a tiny grove not far from Djerba in the south of Tunisia, I was witness to that country's moving tradition of charcoal making. The arid region's charcoal is made from the wood of olive trees past their prime years along with branches cut during trimming. The wood is left to burn for several days in earthen ovens covered with algae and the resulting charcoal is used as cooking fuel. When you realize that in Tunisia the olive is of overwhelming strategic economic importance, you understand the sober ceremonial involved in the process.

The state is very involved in the production process and an enormous system of rather neutral grade oil for export has developed. You also find some small rural units producing poor quality stuff for local markets. It is not easy to find a middle ground, that is, smaller producers of high quality oil.

For some years now certain farms have been privatized, leaving greater flexibility in production options. In the Nabeul region, east of Tunis and south of Cap Bon, a private grower has just obtained an organic food certification for his olives. After having made many trips there, I am

Spread on its blackened pan, a socca *(chickpea pancake)*
combines the rounded flavor of the chickpea with the sharp savor of olive oil.
In Provence, the socca *is eaten hot and well-peppered*
with a glass of chilled Provence white wine.

still amazed by the quality of these olives, called Chemlali. They always seem so healthy, with never a hint of attack by parasites. A modern mill is discreetly installed in a traditional building with a rounded roof and chalk-white walls. The oil has a strong bouquet of pure green apples as it flows out of the press. But you have to wait several days before discovering the full bouquet, because Tunisian oils do not generally have marked aromas. This rather sweet oil marries well with almost any food.

The most remarkable thing about Tunisia is that between the relatively rich and well-watered countryside of vineyards and orchards such as that in the Cap Bon region and the vast near-desert regions around Sfax, the differences in oil taste are quite marked. Between the two types of climatic area, the region of Sousse seems the most likely place for obtaining the best balance the country has to offer. Some Tunisian families in the area are trying to launch quality production operations.

The greatness of olive oil lies in its infinite variety. There is always a new *cru* to discover, a producer to meet, new savors, marriages and mixes to imagine. The world of olives is currently undergoing a renaissance. Mills and ancient groves are being renewed. New groves are being planted throughout the world. For many years to come we will have discoveries to make, new *crus* to appreciate. Treasures of today will be complemented by treasures to come.

Preserved in brine and spiced with herbes de Provence,
these Italian Ascolana olives are prepared by La Cravenco in the Vallée des Baux (above).
The immense olive groves of Morocco (here in the region of Fez) produce a variety of oils,
most of them awaiting discovery (facing page).

A Table in the Sun

In Provence the place to meet is often around a big table. Conviviality here begins in the kitchen, where each friend can bring his or her personal touch to the party by preparing a special dish.

At my table there are old friends like the painter Serge Fiorio. His olives must be taken as an appetizer. Neighbor Nicole Lefort from Mane likes to prepare Middle Eastern mezze, vegetables much to the fore. Chantal Loras, who runs the Paris branches of Oliviers & Co., and the chef Jean-Marie Meulien work the ovens under the keen eye of painter Louis Pons. Writer Pierre Magnan never fails to serve the apéritif while enumerating the merits of his olive oil, always the best there is. And let's not forget Gérard Vives, chef of Lapin Tant Pis in Forcalquier. He loves to come into the cellar to help me choose my wines, talking the while of all the steps involved in making the day's dessert. Then everyone gathers at the table to enjoy the Mediterranean cuisine, enriched with the stories and comments of everyone present.

The recipes that follow arose from these improvised meals with friends and are easy to prepare. My principle of simplicity is borrowed from Michel Biehn's *Le Cahier de Recettes provençales*, a book that, together with my culinary Bible J. B. Reboul's *La Cuisinière Provençale*, never leaves my kitchen.

I have had the pleasure of writing this book with four hands. Two of them were borrowed from one of the greatest chefs of Provence, Jacques Chibois, who has been kind enough to create new recipes for us. My recipes, mere *petits tours de main*, will seem insignificant next to his masterpieces, so I just hope you will take my list as a few salient lines from a gourmet's memoirs, memories of meals that have livened my home and brightened my kitchen in Pierrerue.

Fresh Brousse cheese in Latium olive oil

Dredge a fresh Brousse (a goat's milk cheese) in a mixture of five-grain pepper and sea salt. Splash on Latium or Sardinian olive oil. Accompany with a bowl of corn salad (lamb's lettuce).

Chopped artichoke with Parmesan and Sicilian olive oil

Tear the hardest leaves off a few small, violet artichokes. Cut off the upper part of the

The Andalusian torta, *flavored with olive oil and aniseed, and lightly sugared, is cooked over a wood fire (facing page). The sun is at its highest and the friends will soon be arriving for lunch. On the terrace table, shaded by an attractive trellis, await the mezze prepared by Nicole Lefort in her large home in Mane:* tapenade *and green salad, marinades and anchovy paste, pumpkin pie and baked cod, tomatoes* à la Provençale, *chanterelle mushrooms in vinegar, peppers, eggplant, chickpeas, fresh goat's milk cheeses, garden fruits and olive oils.*

leaves and throw them out. Chop each artichoke in thin slices. Lay the slices in a dish. Splash with lemon juice and let marinate for several hours. Just before serving, salt, pepper and add oil and curls of Parmesan.

Potatoes in saffron and Catalan olive oil

Bake the unpeeled potatoes. Mix together Catalan olive oil and saffron. Pour the mix along with salt and pepper over potatoes just before they are fully cooked.

Olivier Baussan's *brandade* with Istrian olive oil

Brandade is a traditional Provençal casserole of cod and potato. Poach desalted cod in milk for about 10 minutes. Drain. Remove the skin and bones. Boil two unpeeled potatoes. Place the pieces of cod in a steamer or a thick-bottomed cooking pot.

Over a very low fire and using a wooden spoon, work the pieces of cod together, adding a clove of crushed garlic. Then slowly add the Istrian oil. Peel and mash the potatoes and add them. Pepper generously. You should have a thick purée. If it's too thick, add a little liquid cream. Sprinkle on a bit of grated truffle and serve with croutons sautéed in a little olive oil.

Puréed potatoes with Corsican olive oil

Peel and cook potatoes in milk for about 20 minutes. Mash them by hand, slowly adding Corsican oil until you obtain a purée.

Olive oil butter

To spread over slices of toasted bread or summer vegetables. Fill a small dish or bowl with Puglia olive oil. Put it in the freezer for about an hour. Serve with pepper and salt on the side.

Burbot lasagna in a paste of Cailletier black olives

For 4 people, use about 1½ lbs. (800 g) of burbot and a proportional amount of lasagna. Cut the fish into 8 or 16 pieces. Spread on Cailletier black olive paste. Boil 12 cups of lightly salted water (use

*Indispensable for the lighter meal of Christmas Eve, cod baked with leeks (above)
can be eaten with delight the year through: leeks marinated in Haute-Provence olive oil,
blanched and broken cod, some bread crumb, beaten eggs and, for those special occasions,
a few truffles for their inimitable aroma, all covered with breadcrumbs,
sprinkled with olive oil and baked.
Quintessential Mediterranean cuisine: grilled peppers marinated
in Greek or Sicilian oil (facing page).*

sea salt). Boil lasagna for 4 minutes. Remove and drain. Steam the pieces of fish for 5–6 minutes. Put a layer of lasagna in a baking dish. Lay on the burbot. Continue until all ingredients are used. Top layer should be lasagna. Pepper and sprinkle with Parmesan. Bake for a few minutes. Splash on a bit of Nice or Ligurian olive oil just before serving.

Dressing for endive or cabbage

Peel and remove the germ from a clove of garlic. Remove the salt from two salted anchovies by running tap water over them 1 or 2 minutes. Purée garlic and anchovy in a food processor or with a mixer. Add 4 tablespoons of Sicilian olive oil, a dash of lemon juice and a bit of pepper. Mix well. Spread over your salad and toss.

Roasted potatoes

Wash firmly fleshed, unpeeled potatoes (the type you might use for French fries). Lay them in a low-sided baking pan or on a baking sheet. Salt and sprinkle with thyme. Pour Corsican olive oil over them. Heat for about 40 minutes in a fairly hot oven. Serve with a cruet of olive oil and a pepper mill on the side.

Pistou for pasta

Pistou is a garlicky staple in Provence. Peel and remove the germ from 2 cloves of garlic. Purée along with a handful of fresh basil. Salt and pepper the mixture. Add 2 tablespoons of Tuscan olive oil to keep it fluid. Pour the *pistou* over hot spaghetti or other pasta.

Tapenade

A spicy Provençal anchovy spread for toast or a sauce for vegetables. Remove salt from about 2 oz (50 g) of salted anchovy fillets. Purée them along with about 5 oz (150 g) of black olives with pits removed, about 2 oz (50 g) of capers, juice from ½ lemon, pepper and 3 tablespoons of Nyons olive oil. Wonderful with fresh tomatoes.

Fresh tomato *concassé*

Peel and remove seeds from tomatoes. Dice them. Salt, pepper and splash on Sardinian olive oil. Sprinkle with fresh coriander leaves and serve with grilled fish, rice or pasta.

Vegetarian tapas

On each side of a saucer, make a little mound of sea salt and ground pepper. Pour a bit of Umbrian olive oil between them. Serve with branch celery, radishes, cherry

Tapenade, *a purée of black olives, anchovies, garlic and olive oil, is a classic Provençal dish. Eaten on toasted bread with an apéritif, it can also be used as a sauce for grilled mullet or bass.*

tomatoes, sliced fennel, carrot sticks, fresh green beans, artichoke or any vegetable you fancy. Dip the vegetable in the oil, rub it on salt and pepper to taste.

Spaghetti with grated Poutargue cheese

The Poutargue hard cheese is the Provençal cousin of Parmesan. Peel and chop two cloves of garlic and add to a glassful of Sicilian olive oil heating over a low fire. When the garlic has had time to infuse the oil, pour the mixture over *al dente* spaghetti. Generously sprinkle on grated Poutargue and freshly ground pepper. Mix well. Finely grated Parmesan is also delicious.

Sweetened onions for tomato salad

Marinate onions in your favorite olive oil to sweeten their approach to your fresh tomatoes.

Serge Fiorio's green olives

To remove bitterness from olives, soak them in a thick soup of ash and water. Stir several times a day for seven days. When the olives are ready, rinse well with water. Salt, place in canning jars and seal. This simple method doesn't preserve the olives for long, so use them fairly quickly.

Risotto with violet artichokes

Prepare about 4 cups of chicken or beef stock. In a large pot, boil in water with a brimming tablespoon of Latium olive oil a generous 1 lb. (500 g) of uncooked, round Italian rice. When the rice loses its milkiness, add a *bouquet garni* (mixed herbs). Over about 20 minutes—about the time it will take to completely cook the rice—gradually add the stock. Slice about 6 small violet artichokes into fine strips. Sprinkle with lemon juice. Lightly brown in a high-sided frying pan. Turn off the fire. Add chopped garlic and parsley. Slowly stir artichoke strips into rice mixture. Add a splash or two of oil, sprinkle on a bit of grated Parmesan. Serve immediately.

Gérard Vives'cream cheese with raspberries, candied lemon peel and Andalusian olive oil

Mix Mascarpone cream cheese with thick cream. Carefully add in whole raspberries. Place in a cake mold. On top, spread candied lemon rinds along with raspberries. Spread on syrup of basil. Splash on a bit of Andalusian olive oil just before serving.

Delicious Mascarpone cheese with raspberries (facing page),
a light and superbly aromatic dessert from the restaurant Lapin Tant Pis
in the Provençal village of Forcalquier.
To whet gourmet appetites, a pumpkin pie cooling at the window: the pumpkin has been cooked
slowly in Vallée des Baux olive oil, puréed and flavored with orange peel confit
in a little sugared olive oil and mixed with eggs and stiffened egg whites before being laid out
over crust in a pie pan and baked 40 minutes in a medium oven.

Jacques Chibois's Recipes

How did Jacques Chibois, a child of the Limousin and Périgord regions, who studied in Limoges and served his apprenticeship in Paris, end up "falling into" olive oil? "I got a taste for olive oil at the end of the 1970s, in 1979–80, when I was working at Outhier and then at Vergé's," he explains. "Before then I hadn't used it. I hadn't even eaten any." Then Jacques Chibois started working at the Gray d'Albion in Cannes and began to use it in his cooking, which consisted mainly of Mediterranean dishes.

"When I arrived at La Bastide in Grasse I found myself surrounded by olive groves. My attitude began to change. Little by little, without overdoing it or going over the top, I started to use olive oil bought at local mills in my cooking. Then I got to know Olivier Baussan and started taking my experiments a lot further. I've discovered the identity of each oil and just how many of them there are. It has become a game, a daily urge. Just as for wine, there are varieties of olives, regions, climates, techniques, people . . . resulting in different textures, bouquets and flavors. In the end, the discovery of olive oil has influenced my cooking and every time I create a dish I am careful to choose the right oil. It's a pleasure!"

Mushroom, rocket and scallop salad

Salade de champignons, roquette et Saint-Jacques

Serves 4

3 oz. (80 g) rocket
7 oz. (200 g) mushrooms
12 scallops
½ red pepper
8 chopped olives

7 tablespoons Sardinian
olive oil
2 teaspoons lemon juice
1 clove garlic
1 sprig thyme
salt and pepper

*Sardinian olive oil is attractively fruity with
a hint of wildness.*

Wash and dry the rocket. Cut the feet
off the mushrooms and wash them.

Remove the seeds from the pepper and dice.
Remove the pits from the olives and finely dice.
Fill a saucepan with water, pour in the olives
and bring to a boil. Remove the olives. Drain.

Slice the mushrooms finely.

In a frying pan, heat 2 tablespoons of oil along
with the unpeeled clove of garlic and thyme. Salt and
pepper the scallops and add them to the
heated oil, together with the diced pepper
and olives. The scallops need to cook for only
1 minute on each side. When they are done,
add a dash of lemon juice and 1 tablespoon of water
to the contents of the pan.

In a bowl, mix 5 tablespoons of oil and
2 teaspoons of lemon juice. Salt and pepper.
Use half this seasoning on the rocket and half
on the mushrooms.

Make a bed of rocket and mushrooms on the
plates. Lay the scallops over them. Serve warm.

Tuna marinated in Sicilian olive oil
Thon à l'huile d'olive de Sicile

| To be prepared the day before **Serves 4** | 1 lb. (450 g) skinless boneless tuna fillet 1 cup Sicilian olive oil pinch each of thyme, rosemary, savory and marjoram | 2 stalks sweet fennel 2 cloves garlic pinch each of salt and pepper |

In this distinctively Mediterranean dish, the strong and fruity taste of Sicilian olive oil is an excellent match for the tuna.

Court bouillon

Put the herbs and garlic in 1 quart (1 liter) of water and bring to a boil.

Salt and pepper the tuna. In a hot frying pan, add 1 tablespoon of oil and brown the tuna on both sides.

Tuna

Place the tuna in the boiling court bouillon and immediately remove it from the heat and leave to cool: the tuna will cook very slowly. Let it stand until cool.

Drain the tuna, dry it carefully on absorbent paper and put it in a canning jar. Add the herbs (but not the garlic, which may cause fermentation) and the pepper, cover with the olive oil and leave to marinate overnight in the refrigerator.

Serve cold with a salad, tomatoes or grilled peppers.

Chicken marinade with lemon and fresh herbs

Marinade de poulet au citron et herbes fraîches

Serves 4	14 oz. (400 g) white chicken meat 6 tablespoons Catalan olive oil 1 bulb fennel 1 fresh, organic lemon	5 basil leaves 1 stalk dill 4 pinches chives 1 blade citronella 1 stalk tarragon 4 pinches chervil	4 sage leaves 1/2 shallot salt and pepper

Catalan olive oil has a sweet, well-rounded taste, similar to oils from Galilee.

Grate the lemon peel finely.

Marinade

In a bowl, mix the juice from 1/2 the lemon with 5 tablespoons of oil, a pinch of salt, a turn of pepper, the finely chopped shallot, the lemon peel and the shredded herbs. Put aside 1 tablespoon of this sauce for use with the fennel.

Chicken

Heat 1 tablespoon of olive oil in a frying pan. Salt and pepper the chicken. Fry 1 minute per side. Remove and cut into thin slices. Pour on the marinade. Mix well and let it stand 10 minutes.

While the chicken marinates, cut the fennel bulb into small pieces, add the remaining tablespoon of marinade, mix and place on serving plates.

Fry the chicken again on a medium heat, just enough to remove the pink, and arrange it on the plates next to the fennel. Decorate with some whole herbs.

Cold melon soup with tomatoes
Soupe glacée de melon à la tomate

Serves 4

1 melon, about 2 lbs.
(1 kilo)
4 tomatoes
5 tablespoons Andalusian
olive oil
5 basil leaves

1 lemon
salt and pepper

Andalusian olive oil is very fruity and well-rounded.

Peel and remove the seeds from the melon.
Cut about a quarter into small cubes, the rest into
irregular pieces. Peel and remove the seeds
from the tomatoes. Cut 1 of them into small cubes,
the remaining 3 into irregular pieces.

In a frying pan, heat 2 tablespoons of oil.
Salt and pepper the irregular pieces of melon and fry
them, as you would potatoes. Salt and pepper
the tomato pieces (but not the cubes) and add them
to the pan along with the shredded basil. Purée
everything in a food processor with $1/2$ quart (45 cl)
water, some salt, a good amount of pepper
and the juice of the lemon.

Put 2 tablespoons of oil in the frying pan.
Salt and pepper the melon and tomato cubes
and sauté them for 1 minute. Remove from the heat
and let them cool in the pan. When cool, add them
to the soup and put it in the refrigerator to cool
for 1 or 2 hours.

Sprinkle on a bit of olive oil and season
with pepper just before serving.

Lamb's brain terrine and chickpea salad

Terrine de cervelles et sa salade de pois chiches

Serves 6			
	2 lbs. (900 g) lamb's brain	2 bunches parsley	5 tablespoons olive oil
	1 sprig thyme	1 oz. (40 g) small capers	dash of lemon juice
	1 bay leaf	2 lemons	5 basil leaves
	7 oz. (200 g) bread crumb	5 tablespoons Vallée des	1 pinch curry powder
	3 eggs	Baux olive oil	1 teaspoon of balsam
	1 clove garlic	salt and pepper	vinegar
	1 cup liquid cream	salad	salt and pepper
	2/3 cup water	7 oz. (200 g) dried chickpeas	

Vallée des Baux olive oil is well-rounded and lightly spiced, aromatic but with no trace of bitterness.

Chickpea salad

Soak the chickpeas for about 12 hours in a large bowl of cold unsalted water. Then boil them in unsalted water for 1½ hours. Drain. Season with 4 tablespoons of oil, salt and pepper, a dash of lemon juice, balsam vinegar, curry and the shredded basil.

Brain

To clean the lamb's brain, soak it in water for about half a day. Drain and place in a bowl of cold salted water (³/₄ oz. salt per quart of water) with the thyme and bay. Bring to a boil and remove from the heat. The brain cooks as the water cools. Once the water is cool, remove the brain. Drain and cut into cubes of about 1 square inch.

With a mixer, beat together the peeled garlic, parsley, bread, eggs, cream, olive oil, salt and pepper into a smooth paste.

Peel the lemons, being sure to remove all the pieces of white peel, and slice them.

Line a terrine with heat-resistant cooking paper, using enough to make two leaves to fold over as a cover. Pour in a layer of paste and spread on it a layer of brain cubes, a few capers and some pieces of lemon. Continue alternate layers of paste and brain until you have used all the ingredients. The final layer should be of paste. Fold over the covering leaves. Cook in a bain-marie in an oven heated to about 325 °F for 1 hour.

Green bean salad with shrimp, almonds, pine nuts and roasted pistachios

Salade de haricots verts aux petites crevettes, amandes,
pignons et pistaches rôties

| Serves 4 | 14 oz. (400 g) green beans
7 oz. (200 g) small, cleaned shrimp
1^1/2 oz. (40 g) almond slivers | 1^1/2 oz. (40 g) pine nuts
1^1/2 oz. (40 g) shelled pistachios
8 tablespoons Puglia olive oil
2 tablespoons lemon juice | salt and pepper |

The fruity, vegetable taste of Puglia olive oil marries deliciously with green vegetables.

Trim the green beans. Boil for 30 minutes in salted water (1 oz. salt per quart of water). Drain. Plunge them into cold water for 1 second. Drain again.

In a frying pan, add 1 tablespoon of oil. Over a high heat, lightly brown the pine nuts, almonds and pistachios, stirring continuously. Add the shrimp. Remove from the heat and leave to cool 1 minute.

Season the green beans with a mix of 6 tablespoons of oil and 2 tablespoons of lemon juice, together with salt and pepper. Place the beans on serving plates and add the shrimp, pine nuts, almonds and pistachios. Serve immediately.

Truffle salad with pumpkin

Truffle salad au potiron

| Serves 2 | 2/3 oz. (20 g) truffle
9 oz. (250 g) pumpkin (peeled)
1 handful washed, drained lamb's lettuce | 4 tablespoons of Latium olive oil
1 teaspoon of hazelnut oil
1 teaspoon of lemon juice
a few drops balsam vinegar | 1 pinch ground cinnamon
salt and pepper |

Latium olive oil has a full, rounded, long-lasting savor which is a good match for truffles.

Cut up the pumpkin and fry it 5 minutes in 1 tablespoon of olive oil. Season with salt, pepper and a pinch of cinnamon. Take off the heat and sprinkle with hazelnut oil. Leave to cool.

Slice the truffle and mix with lemon juice, 2 tablespoons of oil, a pinch of salt and a turn of the pepper mill.

Mix 1 tablespoon of olive oil with some lemon juice. Pile the lamb's lettuce on 2 serving plates and pour over the lemon-oil mix. At the center of each pile, put half the pumpkin pieces and cover with truffle slices. Add a dash of Latium oil and a few drops of balsam vinegar.

Serve with slices of toast and a bottle of olive oil on the side.

Tomatoes and artichokes with rose petals

Tomates et artichauts aux pétales de rose

Serves 4

4 tomatoes
2 large, precleaned, precooked artichoke hearts
1 handful rose petals
6 tablespoons Pays d'Aix

olive oil
juice from 1/2 a lemon
1 sprig tarragon
salt and pepper

Pays d'Aix olive oil is delicately fruity with a green tomato bouquet.

Peel and quarter the tomatoes. Salt and pepper. Halve the artichoke hearts then cut them into triangles. Salt and pepper.

In a bowl, whip together the oil, lemon juice, salt and pepper. Carefully add half this sauce with the tomato quarters and artichoke. Place on 4 serving plates.

Sprinkle rose petals and tarragon over the tomatoes and artichoke. Sprinkle on the rest of the sauce and serve immediately.

Oysters and sea urchins in almond and lemon jelly with chives

Huitres et oursins en gelée d'amande et citron à la ciboulette

Serves 4

16 medium-size oysters
12 sea urchins
6 strips gelatin
1¼ cups milk
1 cup liquid cream
1 lemon

¾ cup flour
1 drop almond extract
7 tablespoons Catalan
olive oil
a few pinches chives
salt and pepper

Catalan olive oil is sweet with a subtle aroma of almonds.

In a small pan, over low heat, make a béchamel sauce with 1 tablespoon of oil, the flour, salt and pepper. Quickly stir in the hot milk. Let it thicken, stirring continuously for 1 minute after it has boiled. Remove from the heat.

Soften 3 strips of the gelatin in cold water. Drain by pressing. Add them to the béchamel sauce along with the finely grated lemon peel and a few drops of lemon juice. Mix thoroughly. Add a single drop of almond extract. Let the mixture cool, but avoid letting it set.

Whip the cream and add salt and pepper. Whip into the béchamel along with 2 tablespoons of oil. Pour it into the 8 ramekins and put them in a cool place to set.

Open the oysters, taking care to keep the juice. Filter the juice and clean the meat. Put both together in a bowl. Soften the 3 remaining strips of gelatin in cold water. Drain by pressing. Take ⅔ cup of the oyster juice, warm it slightly and put it into a bowl. Add the gelatin. Whip in a dash of lemon juice, 2 tablespoons of oil, some pepper and the rest of the oyster juice. In a small dish, pour this mixture over the oysters. Put in a cool place to set.

Just before serving, remove the almond jelly ramekins from their molds by putting them in boiling water for 1 second. Place the sea urchins on them and arrange the oysters in their jelly around them. Decorate with chives.

Rock lobster salad with orange sauce
Salade de langouste à la bigarade

Serves 4

2 rock lobsters, about 1 lb. (500 g) each	4 tablespoons sherry vinegar	²/3 oz. (25 g) sliced, pan-bleached almonds
5 oz. (150 g) green beans	4 tablespoons wine vinegar	1 orange
5 oz. (150 g) leeks	²/3 cup granulated sugar	1 lemon
²/3 cup Sicilian olive oil		chervil
		salt and pepper

Sicilian olive oil is strong and elegant with a long, distinctive aftertaste.

Cook the lobsters in boiling salted water for 3 to 4 minutes. Drain. Let cool before shelling. Slice the tails into round pieces. Salt and pepper.

Trim the beans. Boil for 6 minutes in salted water (1 oz. salt per quart of water). Cut the leeks lengthwise into four portions and then into ¹/2 inch pieces. Wash and cook for 3 minutes in boiling salted water (³/4 oz. salt per quart of water). Drain and leave to cool.

Prepare the sauce by mixing the olive oil, lemon juice, salt and pepper. Keeping 4 tablespoons of sauce for the lobster, separately season green beans and leeks with it. Finely grate half the lemon peel and add itto the leeks.

Orange sauce

Make the caramel with the sugar and vinegars over a low heat. When it is brown, squeeze on the orange juice. Scrape in a bit of the peel with the tip of a knife. Salt and pepper.

On four serving plates, arrange the leeks and beans next to one another. Put the lobster rounds over the leeks and sprinkle them with the oil-lemon juice mixture and then with the orange sauce. Decorate the dish with chervil, the heads and claws of the lobsters and the sliced, pan-bleached almonds.

Lobster soup
Aigo de homard

Serves 4

2 lobsters	1 cup chicken stock
1 cup good lobster bisque	2/3 cup Manosque olive oil
	2 oz. (60 g) butter
	1/2 lemon
	5 oz. (150 g) diced tomato pulp

6 sage leaves	13/4 oz. (50 g) onion
1 oz. (30 g) seedless black olives	2/3 oz. (20 g) celeriac
8 basil leaves	1 clove garlic
13/4 oz. (50 g) carrots	salt and pepper
13/4 oz. (50 g) green beans	

Olive oil from Manosque in Haute-Provence is full in the mouth with a bouquet of almond and white flowers.

Cook the lobsters in boiling salted water for 3 minutes. Drain and let cool before shelling. Cut the meat into rounds.

Bring the chicken broth to a boil and add the bisque. Season to taste. Dice the carrots, celeriac, green beans and onion and add them to the broth-bisque mixture, together with a clove of garlic. Boil until the vegetables are tender. Strain out the broth-bisque and set the vegetables aside.

In a mixer, purée the broth-bisque, the clove of garlic, butter, olive oil, sage and a dash of lemon juice. Put this soup in a pan and bring to the boil. Arrange the vegetables and lobster pieces in 4 large soup plates. Slice the olives finely and blanch them (to desalt them). Scatter them over the vegetables and lobster, together with the shredded basil. Pour on the hot soup and serve.

Bean soup with sage
Soupe de fèves à la sauge

Serves 4

2¹/₄ lbs. (1 kilo) broad beans
4 tablespoons of Sardinian olive oil
²/₃ cup liquid cream
3 cloves garlic

16 sage leaves
dash of lemon juice
1 small bunch parsley
12 minced black olives
1 teaspoon of coarse-grain salt

pepper
1 quart (1 liter) water

The vegetal bouquet of Sardinian olive oil goes well with this dish, which is both down-to-earth and refined.

Shell the beans and boil them for 1 minute. Remove the pods. Peel the garlic cloves and quarter them.

Add salt to the water and bring to a boil. Add the beans, garlic and 12 sage leaves. Let them boil for 7 minutes. Add the parsley and boil for a further 3 minutes.

With a mixer, purée the soup with 3 tablespoons of olive oil. Add the cream, the remaining sage, 2 or 3 turns of a pepper mill and a splash of lemon juice and mix again.

Serve hot with chopped olives and a splash of olive oil on top.

Ravioli in wine sauce with lamb's feet

Ravioli à la daube et pieds d'agneau

Serves 4

ravioli dough
9 oz. (250 g) flour
4 egg yolks
1 tablespoon Tuscan
olive oil
salt

wine sauce
7 oz. (200 g) stew beef
1 onion
1/2 carrot
2/3 oz. (20 g) celery
1 bouquet garni
2 cloves garlic
2 tablespoons Tuscan
olive oil
1 stalk Swiss chard
2/3 cup white wine

1/3 oz. (10 g) Parmesan
salt and pepper

lamb's feet
8 lamb's feet
5 oz. (150 g) onion
2 1/4 oz. (70 g) carrot
2 cloves garlic
1 tablespoon tomato paste
1 teaspoon coriander
1 teaspoon pepper corns

1 bouquet garni
3 1/4 tablespoons white
wine
1 pinch saffron pistil
4 tablespoons Tuscan
olive oil
salt and pepper
6 basil leaves

*Tuscan olive oil is ideal for enhancing the taste
of both the wine sauce and the ravioli.*

Peel and chop the onion, carrot and garlic.
Heat 4 tablespoons of olive oil in a large oven-safe
cooking pan. Add the onion and carrot and brown
lightly. Add the garlic, tomato paste, saffron, bouquet
garni and white wine, along with pepper and
coriander wrapped in cheesecloth. Add the lamb's
feet, cover with water and bring to a boil. Remove it
from the heat and cook in an oven heated to about
325 °F for 4 hours.

Ravioli and wine sauce
Use an electric mixer to combine the ingredients of
the ravioli dough. If necessary, add a little water to
bring the dough to a workable consistency (firm but
flexible). Roll it in plastic or paper and let it rest 1
hour in a cool place.

For the wine sauce, heat 2 tablespoons of olive oil
in a large cooking pot and brown the pieces of beef
and the sliced onion. Add the sliced carrot and celery
and the crushed garlic. Add the white wine, 3 cups
of water and the bouquet garni. Boil off the water.

Boil the Swiss chard in salted water and dry
thoroughly. When all the liquid has boiled away
from the beef mix, remove it from the heat and take
out the bouquet garni. Grind the beef mix along
with the Swiss chard. Add the Parmesan
and 2 tablespoons of olive oil.

On a floured board, cut the ravioli dough into
equal halves. Roll the halves out as thinly as possible
into 2 rectangles of about the same size. On one
of the rectangles place dabs of the ground beef
at intervals of about 3/4 inch. With a brush, moisten
the remaining rectangle and lay it over the first
rectangle. Flatten the two sheets of dough together
with the side of your hand. Cut out raviolis with
a cutting roller, flour them and lift them off
the board. To cook, bring a large quantity of salted
water to a boil and plunge in the ravioli
for 1 to 2 minutes. Drain.

To serve, take the lamb's feet preparation
from the oven. Remove the feet and place
in a serving dish. Strain the sauce and pour it over
the feet. Add the ravioli, 6 shredded basil leaves
and a dash of olive oil.

Provençale sautéed squid on creamed rice

Calmars sautés à la Provençale sur riz crémeux

Serves 4

7 oz. (200 g) very small pre-dressed squid
6 tablespoons of Vallée des Baux olive oil
2 peeled, diced tomatoes with seeds removed
2 oz. (50 g) grilled, peeled and diced yellow peppers

2 oz. (50 g) minced black olive
6½ tablespoons good lobster bisque
2 tablespoons of liquid cream
1 oz. (25 g) butter
1 sprig shredded tarragon
2 cloves garlic

salt and pepper

creamed rice
7 oz. (200 g) short-grain Spanish rice
1 quart (1 liter) water
2/3 oz. (20 g) coarse-grain salt
2 pinches dehydrated chicken stock

2 tablespoons liquid cream
3 tablespoons freshly grated Parmesan
dash of dry white wine
dash of lemon juice
freshly ground pepper

The aromatic and balanced Vallée des Baux olive oil enhances the rice and stands up well to the squid.

Creamed rice

Bring the salted water to a boil. Add the rice and a pinch of chicken stock. Stir and boil for 10 minutes. Drain thoroughly. To keep the rice from sticking, stir in a tablespoon of olive oil.

In a high-sided frying pan, heat 1¼ cups of water with a pinch of stock, 1 tablespoon of oil, 2 tablespoons of cream, and salt and pepper. Stirring continuously, add the rice. Simmer the mixture while you cook the squid.

Just before you pour the squid and its sauce over the rice, you will add freshly grated Parmesan, a dash of white wine, a dash of lemon and a little pepper.

Squid

Heat 4 tablespoons of oil in a large frying pan. Crush the garlic unpeeled and add it to the oil, along with the squid. After 1 minute add the diced peppers, tomatoes and olives. Stir. Add the tarragon, bisque, cream and butter. Turn the heat up for 1 minute before pouring it over the rice.

To serve, place the rice in a large serving dish and crown it with the squid sauté.

Asparagus with anise
Asperges à l'anis

Serves 4

32 asparagus spears
2 oz. (60 g) Nice black
olives
5 tablespoons Tuscan
olive oil

4 sprigs dill
1²/3 oz. (50 g) butter
1 teaspoon anise grains
¹/2 lemon
salt and pepper

With its delicately vegetal savor, Tuscan olive oil
is strong enough to withstand the anise.

Peel the asparagus with a paring knife. Wash and tie
in a bundle. Boil for 15 minutes in salted water.

While the asparagus cook, prepare the sauce.
In a cooking pot, put ²/3 cup of water, butter, anise,
oil, salt and pepper. Bring to a boil by whipping it
for 1 minute. Remove from the heat. Add a splash of
lemon juice and the olives. Check the seasoning
and pour into a sauceboat.

Drain the asparagus and lay them on a serving
dish. Sprinkle on the dill. Serve the asparagus cool.
Allow the guests to add sauce to taste.

Cep and eggplant cannelloni

Cannellone de cèpes et aubergines

Serves 4	14 oz. (400 g) ceps	$^2/_3$ oz. (20 g) butter	salt and pepper
	14 oz. (400 g) eggplant	5 oz. (150 g) cream	
	8 sheets cannelloni	1 clove garlic	
	2 tablespoons of	1 small bunch parsley	
	Peloponnese olive oil	a few shaves of	
	$^4/_5$ cup chicken stock	Parmesan	

Peloponnese olive oil is rich and smooth, like the cep.

Peel and cut the eggplant into $^1/_2$ inch cubes. Put them in 1 quart (1 liter) cold water in which $1^2/_3$ oz. (50 g) salt has been dissolved for 15 minutes. Drain.

Boil the eggplant for 2 minutes in salted water (2 oz. salt to 1 quart of water). Drain thoroughly.

Soften the sheets of cannelloni in salted boiling water. Drain on a clean towel.

Clean the ceps. Slice them and sauté in butter, salt and pepper. Chop the garlic and half the parsley.

Add them and the eggplant. Mix and cook 5 minutes. Add the cream and bring to a boil. Remove from the heat. Strain out the eggplant and put the strained sauce into a large frying pan. Dilute it with the chicken stock and olive oil and whip it while it comes to the boil. Add the rest of the parsley.

Roll equal amounts of the hot cep-eggplant mix in the cannelloni dough. Arrange the cannelloni in a baking dish and heat a few minutes in the oven before covering with the cooking sauce. Scatter on the Parmesan shavings. Serve immediately.

Pan-fried chanterelle mushrooms with zucchini and gnocchi

Poêlée de chanterelles aux courgettes et gnocchis

Serves 4

14 oz. (400 g)
chanterelle mushrooms
2 small zucchini
1 shallot
Istrian olive oil
2 oz. (60 g) butter

1 small bunch chopped,
rolled parsley
2 cloves garlic
2/3 oz. (20 g) dried ceps
dash of white wine
salt and pepper

gnocchi
9 oz. (250 g) peeled
potatoes
1^1/3 oz. (40 g) flour
1 tablespoon chopped
parsley

Istrian olive oil is complex and pleasantly vegetal.

Gnocchi

Cut the potatoes into pieces and boil them in salted
water. Drain and mash well. Add the parsley and
flour and mix well. Roll the resulting dough
into a long cylinder and cut into sections. Seal each
section by tapping with a fork. Simmer for 3 minutes
in salted water. Drain and sprinkle with olive oil
to keep them from sticking.

Chanterelles and zucchini

Clean the chanterelles. Quarter the zucchini
lengthwise and then cut into smallish triangles.
Peel and chop the shallot and garlic. Chop the
dried ceps finely.

In a large pan, melt half the butter.
Over a high heat, sauté the chanterelles and
the zucchini for 5 minutes. Season. Add the garlic,
shallot, ceps and 2 tablespoons of oil. Stirring often,
continue frying for 1 or 2 minutes. Add 1 cup
of water. Stir. Add the remaining butter and check
the seasoning. Turn the heat to medium and simmer
for 2 minutes. Turn the heat low to keep the mixture
warm. Put in the gnocchi and chopped parsley.
Just before serving, add a dash of white wine.

Socca pancakes and seafood rillettes

La socca et ses rillettes de crustacé

Serves 4

socca
7 oz. (200 g) chickpea
flour
1³/4 cups water

salt and pepper
6 tablespoons Latium olive
oil

seafood rillettes
5 oz. (150 g) shelled shrimp

5 oz. (150 g) crab meat
3 cloves garlic
5 basil leaves
1 sprig thyme
1 small bay leaf

piece of finely grated
lemon peel
4 tablespoons Latium
olive oil
salt and pepper

*Latium olive oil is both refined and strong,
and is rich with aromas.*

Socca

Mix the chickpea flour with the olive oil, water,
salt and pepper. Beat until smooth and let it rest
for 1 hour. Proceed as you would for pancakes,
using generous amounts of oil to keep the soccas
from sticking. Do not turn them. Finish cooking them
under the grill.

Rillettes

Mince the shrimp and crumble the crabmeat.
Mix together.

Peel and halve the garlic. In a frying pan,
over a low heat, heat 5 tablespoons of oil along with
the garlic, bay leaf, thyme, salt and pepper. Let the
oil absorb the flavors of the spices. Add the shrimp
and crab mix and fry for 2 minutes. Remove
the thyme, bay leaf and garlic. Shred the bay leaf and
add it along with the grated lemon peel and a dash
of lemon juice.

Serve each socca hot with a little dome of rillettes
on top. Place the olive oil and lemon slices
on the table.

Roasted gambas with dried herb and asparagus

Gambas rôties aux herbes sèches et aux asperges

Serves 4

12 large gambas 16 green asparagus 1 teaspoon of chopped, dried sage, marjoram and savory (in equal parts)	1 blade citronella 4 basil leaves 1 sprig tarragon 2 cloves garlic 2/3 oz. (20 g) butter	3 tablespoons Sicilian olive oil a few drops of lemon juice 1/2 teaspoon turmeric salt and pepper

Sicilian olive oil is elegant and lively, with a fruity and earthy flavor. Its hint of iodine makes it ideal for gambas.

Peel the asparagus and boil 6 minutes in salted water (1 oz. salt to 1 quart of water). Remove them and plunge immediately into cold water for a few seconds. Drain them and leave them to cool. Cut the bottoms to regularize the lengths. Shape the removed parts into little rounds.

In a frying pan, add all the asparagus with the shredded tarragon, 1 tablespoon of oil, 1/4 cup of water, a pinch of salt and a turn of the pepper mill. Cook on a high heat and let the contents infuse for 1 minute. Add a few drops of lemon juice. Remove from the heat.

Shell the gambas, but do not remove the heads. Salt and pepper. Add a pinch of turmeric on each gamba. Without peeling, crush the garlic. In a frying pan, heat 2 tablespoons of olive oil. Add the garlic, then the gambas. Fry for 2 minutes. Sprinkle on the herb mix, shredded basil and citronella and fry for another 2 minutes. Pour in 2 tablespoons of water to deglaze. Add the sauce from the asparagus.

Arrange the asparagus in a serving dish or on individual plates. Place the gambas on top and pour on the cooking sauce.

Pissaladière with vegetables and olives
Pissaladière aux légumes et aux olives

Serves 4

pie crust
9 oz. (250 g) flour
2 oz. (60 g) softened
butter

6 tablespoons Nice or
Grasse olive oil
2 pinches sugar
5 tablespoons water
salt and pepper

garnish
1 zucchini
1 bulb fennel
4 sweet white or red
onions
1 small eggplant

6 tablespoons Nice or
Grasse olive oil
2 sprigs thyme
12 small Nice black olives
salt and pepper

A sweet Nice or Grasse olive oil adds an appropriately local accent to this dish.

The *pissaladière* is Nice's version of the pizza.

Pie crust
Pile the flour on a pastry board. Make a well in the center and add the salt, sugar, pepper, butter, oil and water. Knead until it has reached a dough consistency. Roll it into a ball and wrap it in pastry plastic or paper. Let it rest 30 minutes in a cool place.

Garnish
While the crust rests, wash, dry and cut the vegetables into strips.

In a frying pan, heat 5 tablespoons of oil and fry the onions for 5 minutes. Salt and pepper the zucchini and add them, together with the eggplant and fennel. Stirring continuously, fry 10 minutes over a fairly high heat. Check the seasoning.

Roll the crust into a rectangle and place it on an oiled pastry sheet. Raise the edges by pinching up. Prick holes in the bottom with a fork.

Pour the vegetable mix into the crust, and sprinkle on the thyme and black olives. Bake at 350 °F for 20 to 25 minutes or until the crust is golden brown. Just before serving, add a splash of olive oil.

Fisherman's mayonnaise
Mayonnaise du pêcheur

Serves 4	½ white onion	2 tomatoes	1 cup Andalusian olive oil
	3½ oz. (100 g) zucchini	1 small bulb fennel	½ tablespoon of Dijon
1 hake, around 2¼ lbs.	3½ oz. (100 g) carrots	3½ oz. (100 g) *penne*	mustard
(1 kilo), scaled and	3½ oz. (100 g) red	9 oz. (250 g) precooked	1 egg
cleaned	peppers	periwinkles	1 sprig tarragon
6½ tablespoons milk	3½ oz. (100 g) green	2 sprigs basil	salt and pepper
1 bay leaf	beans	1 clove garlic	
1 sprig thyme	4 small, firm potatoes	1 lemon	

Andalusian olive oil is ideal for making a savory and distinctive mayonnaise to accompany fish or vegetables.

Vegetables

In a large cooking pot, prepare a court bouillon with 1 quart of water, the milk, thyme, bay, salt and pepper. Put a lid on and let it simmer for 5 minutes. Add the hake. If it is too large to put in whole, cut it into sections. Remove from the heat. The hake will cook in the cooling vegetable broth.

While the fish cooks, peel and wash the vegetables. Boil the potatoes, *penne* and green beans separately in salted water. Drain.

Halve the zucchini and carrots lengthwise and then slice at a slant into pieces. Remove the heart from the fennel and chop it up. Cut the peppers and the onions into pieces. Halve the garlic. In a large frying pan, heat 2 tablespoons of oil and add the zucchini and carrots first and then the other vegetables and garlic. Salt and pepper. Cover and simmer over a low heat for 5 minutes. The vegetables should be crispy.

Remove the outside leaves from the artichokes. Cut off the tops. Chop the hearts and sprinkle them with lemon juice. Quarter the tomatoes. Mix all the vegetables, but not the pasta. Check the seasoning and add 2 tablespoons of oil, a dash of lemon juice and the shredded basil.

Mayonnaise

Mix the yolk with a little of the egg white, the mustard, a dash of lemon juice, and the salt and pepper. Add olive oil and whip vigorously to a mayonnaise consistency. Blend in the shredded tarragon.

Remove the skin from the fish. Using some of the vegetables for a bed, put the fish on a serving dish. Surround it with the remaining vegetables, the periwinkles and *penne*. Put a bit of mayonnaise on the fish and the rest in a serving cup. Decorate with leaves of tarragon and basil.

You may enrich the dish by adding shrimp, rock lobster, whelk or freshly opened mussels.

New wave bass
Loup en nouvelle vague

Serves 4

4 bass fillets, about 5 oz. (150 g) each	2 small zucchini	1 sprig dill
7 tablespoons Catalan olive oil	3 branches dried fennel	2 basil leaves
4 pinches dehydrated chicken stock	4 oz. (120 g) chopped spring onions	2 oz. (60 g) softened butter
	juice of 1 lemon	1/2 clove crushed garlic
	1 vanilla pod	salt and pepper

With its light almond bouquet, Catalan olive oil brings out the fine aromas of this dish.

Sauce

Remove the seeds from the vanilla pod and cut the pod into pieces. Add the seeds and the pod to the oil. Heat at 125 °F for 3 minutes. Put aside.

Chop the onions and sauté with the crushed garlic and fennel for 1 or 2 minutes over a low heat, but don't brown. Then add 1 cup of water, the crushed garlic and the chicken stock. Salt and pepper. Cover and simmer for 10 minutes. Remove the fennel. Whip in the softened butter and a dash of lemon juice. Check the seasoning.

Cut the zucchini into fat, spaghetti-like strips. In a nonstick pan, sauté them in 1 tablespoon of oil. Salt and pepper. Cover, but stir often to avoid browning. After 3 minutes, add the shredded basil and stir. Remove from the heat and set aside.

Fry the bass in 1 tablespoon of oil for 1 or 2 minutes on each side, depending on thickness. Salt and pepper.

Arrange the zucchini strips on serving plates. Put the bass on top. Squeeze lemon juice over each fillet and pour vegetable sauce on top. Sprinkle a bit of oil over each.

Mullet with tomatoes, saffron-seasoned olive oil and sesame

Rougets à la tomate, huile d'olive safranée, graines de sésame

Serves 4

12 Mediterranean mullet of about 2 oz. (60 g) each, or 8 of about 3 oz. (90–100 g)

6 large, peeled, finely diced tomatoes
1 chopped sweet onion
4 cloves garlic
6 tablespoons Andalusian olive oil

3 knife tips of ground saffron
3 knife tips paprika
1 sprig rosemary
1 sprig thyme
1 tablespoon pan-fried

sesame seeds
1/2 lemon
salt and pepper

Andalusian oil is as savory on the firm, tasty meat of the mullet as it is on the acid tomatoes.

Over a low heat, warm the paprika and saffron in 3 tablespoons of oil. Remove from the heat and set aside to infuse.

Prepare the *tomates concassées* by heating 3 tablespoons of non-infused oil in a cooking pot. Fry the onions, diced tomatoes, 2 cloves of crushed garlic, thyme, half the rosemary, and salt and pepper. Let simmer for 5 minutes.

In a frying pan, heat the infused oil. Cut 2 cloves of garlic into quarters and add to the oil, along with the remaining rosemary. Mix. Salt and pepper the mullet. Fry it over a low heat for 2 or 3 minutes on each side, depending on size. When done, squeeze a bit of lemon juice on each one.

Pile the *tomates concassées* on each serving plate and place the mullet on top. Sprinkle with sesame seeds and olive oil.

Homemade salt cod in purée
with olive oil and olives
Morue maison purée à l'huile d'olive et aux olives

Serves 4

1¼ lbs. (600 g) fresh cod
in 4 pieces
2 lbs. (1 kilo) coarse-
grain salt
²/₃ oz. (20 g) sugar

1 tablespoon juniper
berries
2 lbs. (1 kilo) potatoes
(Monalisa variety)
1³/4 oz. (50 g) seedless
green olives

1³/4 oz. (50 g) seedless
black olives
½ lemon
7 tablespoons Corsican
olive oil

*An ample flavor and hint of bitterness makes
Corsican olive oil an ideal accompaniment for potato.*

Mix the salt, sugar and juniper. Roll the cod
in the mixture, patting it so that it becomes thoroughly
impregnated. Put it aside 1 hour in a cool place.
Rinse and steep the cod in cold water for 10 or 15
minutes depending on the size of the pieces.

Peel and boil the potatoes in salted water
(1 tablespoon salt per quart of water). When soft, drain.
Add 5 tablespoons of oil and crush well with a fork.
Slice the black olives, scald and add to the purée.

In 2 tablespoons of oil, fry the cod, skin side
first. When the skin is brown, turn and cook for
2 or 3 minutes.

Lay the cod over the purée and scatter the sliced,
pitted, scalded green olives over it. Sprinkle the cod
with lemon juice and a little fresh oil.

Scampi and eggplant with olives in the Grasse style
Langoustines aux aubergines en grassoise d'olives

Serves 4	6 sprigs dried fennel or a tablespoon of fennel seed	1 lb. (500 g) eggplant
20 scampi	$^4/_5$ cup liquid cream	1 lemon
2 tablespoons chopped	2 oz. (60 g) butter	3 oz. (100 g) fine salt
black olives blanched	6 tablespoons Sicilian	1 clove garlic
twice	olive oil	pepper

With its vegetal bouquet, its hint of iodine and its strength, Sicilian olive oil stands up well to the fennel without overwhelming the scampi.

Peel and dice the eggplant into   inch cubes. Place it in cold salted water ($2^1/_2$ tablespoons salt per quart of water) for 15 minutes, then drain. Boil for 2 minutes in salted water ($1^1/_2$ tablespoons salt per quart of water) and drain for 15 minutes. Fry it lightly in a frying pan with 1 tablespoon of oil and $^1/_2$ tablespoon of butter. Stir with a fork on which you have speared a clove of garlic. Season with a turn of the pepper mill. Check the seasoning. Remove from the heat.

To infuse the cream, heat it over a low heat with the fennel, making sure it doesn't boil. Strain out the fennel, then whip in the rest of the butter and 2 tablespoons of olive oil. Salt and pepper. Grate in the peel from half a lemon and a few drops of lemon juice. Add the chopped olives.

Shell the scampi, keeping 4 heads. Salt and pepper the tails. Brown rapidly in hot olive oil. Boil the 4 heads in salted water.

Arrange the eggplant in a serving dish and place the scampi tails on it. Decorate with the heads. Serve the sauce on the side.

Burbot in minestrone with lima beans

Lotte en minestrone aux cocos

Serves 4

4 small burbot, heads removed
5 oz. (150 g) fresh lima beans

1³/4 oz. (50 g) very small smoked lardons
1 medium-size sweet onion
1 zucchini
1 carrot
2/3 oz. (20 g) celeriac

5 tablespoons Peloponnese olive oil
2/3 oz. (20 g) butter
1 sprig thyme
1/2 bay leaf
5 basil leaves

1 small bunch rolled parsley
2 cloves garlic
1/2 tomato
1/2 cup small Nice olives
salt and pepper

Rich and smooth, Peloponnese olive oil marries well with both the burbot and the lima beans.

Peel the onion, carrot and celeriac. Wash and dry. Dice them into very small cubes. In a pan, melt and mix 1/2 of the butter and 2 tablespoons of oil. Lightly brown the vegetables. Salt and pepper. Add the beans, 2 cups of water, the thyme, the bay, 1 peeled, chopped garlic clove and 1/2 peeled, diced tomato with the seeds removed. Cover and simmer for 15 minutes.

Dice the zucchini into small cubes and add it to the vegetables, along with the olives.

Salt and pepper the burbot. In a frying pan, heat 2 tablespoons of oil with the lardons and the unpeeled, crushed garlic clove. Brown the burbot on both sides, but don't fry for longer than 2 or 3 minutes. Remove from the pan. On a high heat, add 3 tablespoons of water to the pan to deglaze. Add the remaining butter, the parsley and the shredded basil. Check the seasoning. Remove the garlic. Pour this sauce over the beans.

Put the beans in a serving dish topped with the burbot. Sprinkle on the olive oil and serve immediately.

Mediterranean sea bream with almonds and scented with garden flowers

Dorade de Méditerranée aux amandes et senteurs de fleurs de jardin

Serves 4

4 bream fillets, about
5 oz. (150 g) each
1 onion
1 clove garlic

2 stalks dried fennel
2 tablespoons sliced
almonds
1 small handful of rose,
wisteria, acacia,
nasturtium, violet, broom

or other aromatic petals
1 zucchini
5 oz. (150 g) green
beans
a few pinches fresh
coriander

1 teaspoon fennel grains
8 tablespoons Catalan
olive oil
1 lemon
salt and pepper

The rather sweet flavor of the Catalan olive oil, with its hint of almond, enhances the refined savor of the bream.

Soften the onion briefly in 4 tablespoons of oil. Add 1 cup of water and the peeled, chopped garlic, fennel, salt and pepper. Simmer for 15 minutes. Remove the fennel. Pour the sauce into a mixing bowl. Add 2 tablespoons of oil, 1 teaspoon of grated lemon peel and a few drops of lemon juice. Blend and pour into a cooking pan. Add the fennel grains and infuse for 1 minute over a medium heat.

Boil the green beans in salted water (1 tablespoon salt per quart of water). Cut the zucchini into sticks and do the same for them. Drain them before they become soft.

Salt and pepper the bream and fry in 2 tablespoons of oil. Sprinkle with lemon juice.

Shred the coriander and add it to the sauce. On serving plates, make a bed of zucchini and green beans and add a little sauce. Lay on the bream. Mix the almonds and flower petals together and sprinkle over the vegetables and fish. Serve the rest of the sauce on the side.

Plaice with spelt and lardons

Sole rôtie, épeautre aux lardons en rouge et noir

Serves 4

2 large plaice, 1¼ lbs. (600 g) each	4 tablespoons Latium olive oil	1 tablespoon diced, scalded black olives
5 oz. (150 g) spelt	1 tablespoon aged wine vinegar	1 knife tip ground cinnamon
3 oz. (90 g) smoked lardons	1 tablespoon diced red pepper	1 knife tip allspice
3¼ oz. (100 g) carrots		salt and pepper
1 shallot		

The fine but intense savor of Latium olive oil gives the spelt a delicious flavor.

Soak the spelt for 12 hours and then boil it for 1 hour in 1 quart of water. Salt when done.

Remove the heads from the plaice and cut the fish lengthwise. In a large frying pan, heat the lardons in 2 tablespoons of oil. Add the plaice and brown on each side for 2 or 3 minutes, according to thickness. Remove the fish and keep warm on a plate covered with aluminum foil.

Grate the carrots and brown them in the frying pan. Chop the shallot. Add it and then deglaze with, first, vinegar and then with 1¼ cups of water. Heat to reduce volume by half.

Once the spelt is done, mix in 2 tablespoons of oil, the diced pepper and black olives, the cinnamon and allspice. Check the seasoning. Let the water evaporate a little so that the spelt is not too wet.

Make a bed of spelt on each serving plate. Lay on the pieces of plaice and cover with fried carrots and lardons.

Baked sea bream with fennel, tomato and artichoke

Pageot au four, fenouil, tomate et artichaut

Serves 4

1 large sea bream, about 2½ lbs. (1.2 kilos)
2 tomatoes
1 fennel bulb
4 baby artichokes
1 sweet onion

3 cloves garlic
5 or 6 branches dried fennel
3 tablespoons Sicilian olive oil
salt and pepper

Fruity Sicilian olive oil has a hint of iodine that heightens the flavor of the fish.

Salt and pepper the fish. Quarter the fennel bulb, remove the heart and tear the fennel leaves into irregular pieces. Peel and slice the onions and garlic. Cut the artichoke stems to 2 inches. Remove the large leaves and trim the tips of the others with a paring knife. Remove the spines. Halve the hearts and cut into fine slices.

In a frying pan, heat 4 tablespoons of olive oil. Fry the onion and artichoke slices over a high heat. Salt and pepper. Simmer for 5 minutes. Add the garlic. Quarter the tomatoes and add in. Stir. Pour in 1 cup of water.

Break up 1 branch of fennel. Scatter the pieces over the fish and sprinkle with olive oil. In a baking dish, arrange the remaining fennel branches and pour in the vegetables with their sauce. Lay on the fish and sprinkle with olive oil. Cover with aluminum foil, being sure to cover completely, including the tails.

Bake the fish for 15 minutes in an oven at 350 °F. Serve in a baking dish with olive oil and lemon juice on the side.

John Dory with citronella
Saint-Pierre à la citronnelle

Serves 4

2 John Dory fish,
about 1¹/4 lbs. (600 g) each
8 tablespoons Sicilian olive
oil

6 blades citronella
2 lbs. (1 kilo) young spinach
1 lemon
1 cup liquid cream
1³/4 oz. (50 g) softened
butter

1 tablespoon white wine
3 tablespoons Noilly Prat
(vermouth)
1 tablespoon chopped
shallot
1 small bunch dill

1³/4 oz. (50 g) cucumber
1 clove garlic
salt and pepper

Sicilian olive oil is both fruity and earthy, with
hints of iodine and lemon.

Wash the spinach and dry thoroughly.

In a baking dish, pour 2 tablespoons of oil
and lay on 4 blades of citronella. Lay the John Dory
over the citronella. Salt and pepper. Sprinkle the
olive oil. Bake at 350 °F.

While the fish cooks, prepare the sauce. In a
high-sided frying pan, add the shallot, the Noilly Prat
and the white wine. Reduce by half, then add
the cream along with the finely chopped citronella
and the salt and pepper. Simmer for a good
5 minutes. Whip in the butter, 2 tablespoons of olive
oil and a dash of lemon juice, then add the diced
cucumber.

In a large frying pan, reduce the spinach
in 2 tablespoons of olive oil. Rub the tines of a fork
with a clove of garlic and use it to stir.

Serve the John Dory in its baking dish. Decorate
with dill. Serve the spinach and sauce apart.

Chicken breast with endive and beets
Poulet aux endives et à la betterave

Serves 4

4 chicken breasts
6 endives
1 small, uncooked beet

3 tablespoons
Peloponnese olive oil
1 knife tip curry powder
6 1/2 tablespoons liquid
cream
2 tablespoons vermouth

1 2/3 oz. (50 g) softened
butter
1 shallot
1 teaspoon vinegar
1 lemon

1 tablespoon chopped
chives
salt and pepper

Fruity Peloponnese olive oil is silky and full in the mouth.

Quarter the endives and cut into 1/2-inch-wide sections. Stirring often, reduce until caramelized in 2 tablespoons of oil. Season with salt and pepper. When well-browned, deglaze with vermouth and cream. Add the curry powder. Simmer a few minutes to thicken.

Dice the beet into small cubes. Sauté in 1 tablespoon of oil. Salt and pepper. Cover and cook for

10 minutes, stirring often. Chop up the shallot and brown it with the beets. Deglaze with vinegar and 1/2 cup of water. Reduce by half. Whip in the butter, 2 tablespoons of oil and the chives.

Salt and pepper the chicken breasts. In 2 tablespoons of oil, over a low heat, cover and fry for 8 to 10 minutes, turning 4 times.

Serve the chicken over a bed of endives. Serve the sauce separately.

Calf's liver with artichoke purée

Foie de veau à la purée d'artichaut

Serves 4

2 thick slices of calf's liver, about 10 oz. (300 g) each
4 large artichokes

7 tablespoons Tuscan olive oil
1/2 tablespoon sherry vinegar
3 tablespoons liquid cream

1 teaspoon Provence honey
1 tablespoon coriander
2 tablespoons tamari (organic soya) sauce

1 teaspoon balsam vinegar
1³/5 oz. (50 g) butter
salt and pepper

Tuscan olive oil enhances the artichoke without masking the delicate richness of the liver.

Break off the artichoke stems to remove the fibers. Boil them in salted water (1 tablespoon salt per quart of water) for 20 to 30 minutes, depending on their size. The hearts should be thoroughly cooked.

Remove the leaves from the artichokes and scrape the edible part from the base. Remove the spines from the hearts. Purée the flesh with 3 tablespoons of oil, 1/2 tablespoon of sherry vinegar, 4 tablespoons of water, the cream, and the salt and pepper.

Salt and pepper the liver. Fry in 2 tablespoons of oil for about 15 minutes, turning when half done.

Prepare the sauce while the liver is frying. In a pan, put the honey, tamari sauce, coriander, 2 tablespoons of oil, 3 tablespoons of water, salt, pepper and butter. Whip as the sauce heats. Add the remaining vinegar.

Serve the liver sliced, accompanied by the purée. Serve the sauce separately.

Pigeon with polenta

Pigeon à la polenta

Serves 4

2 large pigeons
3 tablespoons Vallée des
Baux olive oil
1 oz. (30 g) mixed dried
morel and *trompettes de
la mort* mushrooms

1 shallot
3 tablespoons organic
tamari sauce
1 teaspoon cognac
2 teaspoons port
salt and pepper

polenta
9 oz. (250 g) fine
cornmeal
1 pinch dehydrated
chicken stock
1 pinch ground cumin
4 tablespoons liquid
cream

5 tablespoons Vallée
des Baux olive oil
salt and pepper

*The aromatic and smooth Vallée des Baux olive oil brings
out the flavor of the polenta and enlivens the pigeon.*

Prepare the sauce. Slice the dried mushrooms finely.
Wash them twice to rinse out the earth. Let them dry
thoroughly. Heat 1 tablespoon of oil in a saucepan
over a low heat, and sauté the chopped shallot.
Add the mushrooms, cognac, port, 1 cup of water
and tamari and cook for 10 minutes.

Halve the pigeons. Remove the spine and wings.
Salt and pepper. In two tablespoons of olive oil,
brown the halves on the skin side and leave to cook
for 4 to 5 minutes. Add the wings, also on the skin
side, over a fairly high heat. Turn at the end of
5 minutes. Remove from heat.

Polenta

Boil 1 quart of water with ½ oz. (12 g) of salt,
the cumin and the chicken stock. Remove from
the heat and, stirring vigorously, pour in the cornmeal.
Put it back on a low heat, cover and cook for 5
minutes, stirring from time to time with a spatula.
Add the cream and 5 tablespoons of oil.

Make a bed of polenta and lay on the pigeons.
Pour on the mushroom sauce.

Licorice duckling with potatoes, peppers and onions

Canette confite à la réglisse poêlée de pommes de terre, poivrons et oignons

Serves 4–6

2 ducklings
1 ground licorice tip
14 oz. (400 g) firm
potatoes
1 red pepper
1 large red onion

4 tablespoons Istrian
olive oil
1 splash lemon juice
5 tablespoons dry white
wine
salt and pepper

*Istrian olive oil is rich and strong, marrying well
with the flavor of the licorice.*

Have the butcher dress the ducks. Be sure to keep
the giblets. Salt and pepper them and place them
in a metal roasting pan surrounded by the giblets.
Cook them at about 325 °F for 1¹/₂ hours.

Peel the potatoes and quarter them. Remove
the seeds from the pepper and peel the onion.
Cut both into pieces. In a large frying pan, heat
4 tablespoons of oil and fry the potatoes. When
browned, add the pepper and the onion pieces.
Salt and pepper. Cook for 15 minutes.

When the ducks are done, remove them from
the pan. Keep them warm in another receptacle.
Skim the fat from the juice that remains in the
roasting pan and put the pan on the heat. Add the
white wine. Reduce a little and then add 2 cups of
water. Reduce the volume by half and pour into
a cooking pot. Add the licorice tip and a dash of
lemon juice. Pour this sauce over the potatoes
and boil for 1 minute.

Carve the ducklings and place the pieces
on the vegetables.

Saddle of lamb with stewed fennel, sausage, lardons and thyme flowers

Carré d'agneau à la fondue de fenouil, saucisson, lardons et fleurs de thym

Serves 4

saddle of lamb, about
1²/3 lbs. (800 g)
1³/4 oz. (50 g) finely
sliced garlic sausage
1³/4 oz. (50 g) very small
lardons

4 bulbs fennel
½ sweet onion
1 clove unpeeled garlic
3 tablespoons
Haute-Provence olive oil
2 sprigs thyme

1 pinch thyme flowers
1 pinch ground cumin
salt and pepper

Haute-Provence oil is both sweet and aromatic.

Quarter the fennel bulbs. Remove the hearts and mince the leaves. Boil them in salted water (1 tablespoon salt per quart of water) for 6 minutes. Drain. Recrisp by plunging them into cold water and draining again.

Cut the sausage into fine strips.

Salt the lamb. Put it in a roasting pan with 1 tablespoon of oil, 1 clove of unpeeled crushed garlic and 2 sprigs of thyme. Roast at 400 °F for 12 minutes. Remove the lamb from the pan, place on a grill and cover with aluminum foil.

In a frying pan, heat 2 tablespoons of oil and sauté the chopped onion and the lardons. When the onion is a golden color, add the sausage and then the fennel, thyme flower and cumin. Simmer for 5 minutes.

Reheat the lamb for 5 minutes at 425 °F. Serve hot with the vegetables.

Young rabbit stewed *à la Provençale* with sautéed potatoes

Lapereau rôti en Provençale, sauté de pommes de terre

Serves 4	1 cup shelled, precooked	4 stalks rolled parsley	2 tablespoons white
	young broad beans	1 sprig savory	wine
1 young rabbit, about	6 tablespoons	4 sage leaves	1³/4 oz. (50 g) butter
2¹/3 lbs. (1.2 kilos)	Haute-Provence olive oil	1 sprig rosemary	salt and pepper
2 small zucchini	6 cloves garlic	1 sprig thyme	
4 charlotte potatoes	1 small onion	1 bay leaf	

Provence oil from the Massif des Maures with its slightly spicy savor blends well with this dish.

Cut up the rabbit so as to have 4 pieces of saddle along with the thighs and legs. Halve the kidneys and liver.

Peel and wash the potatoes. Wash the zucchini and parsley. Peel the onion and garlic.

Cut each potato in six and dry. In a nonstick frying pan, heat a tablespoon of oil and add the potatoes. Salt and pepper. Fry over a medium heat until tender and brown.

Cut the zucchini into pieces and fry in 1 tablespoon of oil. Salt and pepper.

Put the potatoes and zucchini in a pan. Add the butter, quarter garlic cloves, thyme, rosemary, bay leaf and savory. Stir and leave for 1 or 2 minutes so that the potatoes absorb the herbal flavors. Remove the garlic and the herbs and put them aside for later use.

Salt and pepper the rabbit. Heat 2 tablespoons of oil in a large cooking pot on a high heat and brown the rabbit, stirring often, for 5 minutes. Turn down the heat. Chop the onion and add it to the rabbit. Simmer for 5 minutes. Add the white wine and garlic. Reduce the volume for 3 minutes. Add ²/3 cup of water and the herbs that have been kept aside. Cover and simmer for 5 minutes. Add all the vegetables, including the beans. Shred the remaining sage and the parsley and add. Stir, and add a dash of olive oil. Remove the thyme, savory, rosemary and bay leaf. Serve hot off the stove.

Quail with cabbage and dried figs

Cailles au chou et aux figues

Serves 4	1³/4 oz. (50 g) celery	5 tablespoons cognac	1³/4 oz. (50 g) butter
	4 dried figs	2 cups red wine	salt and pepper
6 large quails	1 clove garlic	1 pinch dehydrated	
1 small green cabbage	1 small bouquet garni	beef stock	
5 oz. (150 g) onions	a few crushed	6 tablespoons Corsican	
3¹/2 oz. (100 g) carrots	peppercorns	olive oil	

*The rather gamey taste of Corsican olive oil suits
this sweet and sour dish well.*

Have the butcher prepare the quails, halving
the carcass. Keep the wing tips, liver, neck and spine.

Marinade

Peel and dice the carrots, onions and celery.
In a frying pan, heat 2 tablespoons of oil and sauté.
Salt and pepper. Deglaze with red wine. Add the
bouquet garni. Chop the garlic and add it,
together with the crushed peppercorns, dehydrated
beef stock and salt and pepper. Simmer 5 minutes.
Remove from the heat to cool.

Cut off the leafy parts from the stems of the
cabbage. Boil the leaves in salted water (1 tablespoon
salt per quart of water) for 6 minutes. Drain.

Cut the figs in half, then into slices. In a frying pan,
fry them in 1 tablespoon of oil with ¹/3 of the onion.
When the onion is golden brown, pour in ¹/2 cup of
water. Reduce by half. Add the cabbage along with
2 tablespoons of oil. Stirring often, cook the cabbage
for 2 or 3 minutes. Remove from the heat.

When the marinade is cool, pour it over
the quails and their giblets. Leave it to marinate
for 15 minutes.

Quails

Drain the quails and giblets and pat dry with a
paper towel.

In a tablespoon of oil, over a high heat, sauté
the giblets, wing tips, neck and spine. When the meat
takes color, pour on the cognac and light. Add the
marinade with the vegetables and a cup of water.
Simmer for 15 minutes. Strain out the vegetables.
Reduce the liquid volume to a bit less than ¹/2 cup.
Whip in the butter and 2 tablespoons of oil. Check
the seasoning.

Salt and pepper the quails. Fry skin side down
over a high heat for 5 minutes. Turn and cook a bit
longer.

Serve the quails over a bed of cabbage covered
with the vegetable sauce.

Peppered beef fillet with stewed vegetables

Filet de boeuf au poivre et compotée de légumes

Serves 4

fillets
1¼ lbs. (600 g) beef
fillet, cut and rolled into
4 tournedos
18 firm-fleshed black
olives

1 tablespoon coarse-
ground pepper
5 basil leaves

*for the stewed
vegetables*
7 oz. (200 g) stew beef
3 carrots

½ bulb fennel
1 zucchini
9 oz. (250 g) firm
potatoes
16 small Nice black olives
7 tablespoons Corsican
olive oil
1 bay leaf

1 sprig thyme
1 small stalk rosemary
1 clove garlic
2/3 cup red wine
3¼ tablespoons port
salt and pepper

*Corsican oil has enough native character to make
a successful marriage with the pepper in this dish.*

Vegetables

Cut the stew beef into small pieces. Peel the onion
and cut into pieces. In a large pan, heat 4 tablespoons
of oil. Brown the beef and onion. Peel and slice
the carrots in thick diagonal sections and add. Let
the carrots brown a bit. Pour in the red wine and port.
Reduce the liquid volume by half. Add 3 cups of water.
Chop and add the garlic, along with the thyme, bay
leaf, rosemary, Nice olives, salt and pepper. Simmer
1 hour. Remove the thyme, bay leaf and rosemary.

In a frying pan, brown the potatoes in 2 tablespoons
of oil. Chop the fennel and zucchini and add.
Brown 3 minutes. Pour the contents of the pan
into the cooking pot and stir.

Beef tournedos

Remove the stones, chop and scald the black olives.
Drain thoroughly. Chop the basil and add it along
with the pepper to the olives.

Roll the tournedos in the mixture, pressing hard
to make it stick. Fry in 1 tablespoon of oil.
Serve them over stewed vegetables.

Saddle of veal with green olives and Swiss chard

Carré de veau en cocotte aux olives vertes et blettes

Serves 4

1 slab veal saddle,
about 2 lbs. (1 kilo)
3¹/2 oz. (100 g) green
olives
1 large bunch Swiss
chard

¹/2 sweet onion
1 clove garlic
1 pinch dehydrated
chicken stock
1 piece mace
1¹/4 oz. (40 g) butter

6 tablespoons Tuscan
olive oil
salt and pepper

Tuscan oil has a lovely bouquet but is in no way aggressive.

Salt and pepper the veal. In a large cast iron roasting pan, heat 1 tablespoon of oil and brown. Place the pan in an oven heated to 400 °F for 20 minutes. After 10 minutes, add the chopped onion. When the onion has softened, add 1 cup of water. When the time is up, remove the veal from the pan, put it on a grill and cover with aluminum foil. Let it cool 30 minutes.

Remove the stones from the olives. Slice, scald and drain them.

Cut the green leaves from the stems of the chard and cut the stems in sections. Wash and drain. In a frying pan, heat 2 tablespoons of oil and cook the chard for about 15 minutes over a medium heat. About midpoint, cut the garlic clove in two and add, along with the chicken stock.

Put the roasting pan over a heat and add the mace and olives. Stir and simmer 3 minutes. Remove the mace. Whip in 3 tablespoons of oil and butter. Sprinkle the lemon juice to finish.

Just before serving, put the veal in the oven (400 °F) for 5 minutes. Place the veal on the vegetables and serve the sauce separately.

Braised pork ribs with herbs cooked in potter's clay

Etouffé d'échine de porc aux herbes, cuite en argile

Serves 4

ribs
1²/₃ lbs. (800 g) pork ribs
2 cloves garlic
2 tablespoons Istrian
olive oil
2 stalks rosemary

2 stalks thyme
2 stalks savory
4 sage leaves
2 lbs. (1 kilo) potter's clay
salt and pepper

vegetables
1 heart radioso lettuce
1 lb. (200 g) celeriac
6 tablespoons Istrian
olive oil
salt and pepper

sauce
1 sweet onion
³/₄ oz. (25 g) butter
4 tablespoons Istrian
olive oil
1 splash walnut oil
salt and pepper

Istrian olive oil marries perfectly with pork.

Ribs

Brown the pork on all sides in 2 tablespoons of oil.
Salt and pepper.

Roll out the potter's clay as you might do
for pie crust. Lay on the ribs and herbs. Seal in
the ribs and put in a roasting pan. Cook at 325 °F
for 1¹/₂ hours.

While the pork cooks, prepare the vegetables.
Slice the celery to obtain strips the thickness
of tagliatelli 2¹/₂ to 4 inches long. Salt and pepper.
In a frying pan in 2 tablespoons of oil, cover
and cook the celery for 8 to 10 minutes, stirring
frequently.

Cut the turnips into thin slices. Salt and pepper.
In 2 tablespoons of oil, cook covered for 8 to 10
minutes, stirring often.

Wash the lettuce heart and quarter it.
Brown in 2 tablespoons of oil. Salt and pepper.

Rib sauce

Peel and chop the onion. Brown in 2 tablespoons of oil
with salt and pepper. When the onion has a golden
hue, pour in ⁴/₅ cup of water. Reduce the volume
by half. Strain. Put the vegetables aside and stir in
the butter and 2 tablespoons of oil. Check the seasoning.
Just before serving, add a dash of walnut oil.

Serve the pork in its clay casing. Serve the
vegetables and rib sauce on the side.

Strawberry duo in olive oil infused with vanilla

Duo de fraises à l'huile d'olive vanillée

Serves 4

14 oz. (400 g)
strawberries
7 oz. (200 g) wild
strawberries
3 tablespoons Sicilian
olive oil

1 pod vanilla
1 lime
1¼ oz. (40 g) sugar

The fruity refinement of Sicilian olive oil marries well with the flavor of vanilla and lime, bringing out the best of the exotic flavors.

Halve the vanilla pod. Scrape out the grains and put them in a small cooking pan with the oil. Cut the pod into pieces and add it. Warm the oil at not more than 120 °F for 3 minutes. Remove from the heat and let it infuse as it cools.

Wash rapidly, dry and hull the strawberries (wild strawberries should not be washed and will have already been hulled). Arrange all the berries on serving plates (white ones bring out the golden hues of the oil best).

Wash and dry the lime. Grate the peel very finely (as you might for Parmesan). Mix it with the sugar and sprinkle on the strawberries. Add a dash of freshly squeezed lemon juice. Pour the olive oil over the strawberries. You may wish to enrich with a scoop of cherry or raspberry sherbet.

Frozen cream with olive oil and figs in spiced wine syrup

Glace à l'huile d'olive, figues au vin et aux épices

Serves 4

12 figs
cold cream
2 cups milk
9 oz. (250 g) heavy cream

5 oz. (150 g) sugar
5 egg yolks
6½ tablespoons Catalan
olive oil
1 pod vanilla

wine syrup
2 cups red wine
1²/3 oz. (50 g) sugar
½ pod vanilla
peel of ½ orange
½ stick vanilla

1 knife tip ground
saffron

Catalan olive oil is sweet and full, with a hint of almonds.

Frozen cream

Heat the milk and cream together. Halve the vanilla pod and add it. In a large bowl, beat the egg yolks and sugar together to obtain a clear and frothy consistency. Bit by bit, beating with a wooden spoon the while, pour in the milk and cream. Put on a very low heat. Continue stirring until the mixture begins to stick to the spoon. Pour in the olive oil. Remove from the heat and leave to cool. Put in the freezer to firm.

Figs

For the figs, make a syrup. In a cooking pan, bring to a boil the wine, sugar, orange peel, split vanilla pod, cinnamon and saffron. Add the figs. Turn the heat to low and simmer for 15 minutes. Remove from the heat and leave to cool. Remove the figs. Put the syrup back on the heat. Reduce the volume until it is thick. Put the figs back in to get them hot.

To serve, lay the hot figs in soup plates and pour on the syrup. Put a dollop or two of cold cream to the side.

Pumpkin fritters with olive oil, lemon and orange peel

Beignets de potiron à l'huile d'olive, zestes de citron et orange

Serves 4

pumpkin
14 oz. (400 g) sliced pumpkin
3 cups frying oil
2 tablespoons granulated sugar

½ teaspoon ground cinnamon
1 orange peel
1 lemon peel
confectioners' sugar

fritter batter
9 oz. (250 g) flour

2 egg yolks
2 beaten egg whites
6 tablespoons sugar
½ teaspoon salt
2 cups milk
1 tablespoon baking soda
1 lemon peel

1 orange peel
½ teaspoon ground cinnamon
2 tablespoons Catalan olive oil

Catalan olive oil is sweet with a hint of almonds.

Fritter batter

Mix the flour, salt, sugar, baking soda, cinnamon, egg yolks and finely grated lemon and orange peels. Slowly work in the olive oil. Let it stand for 1 hour in a cool place. Just before using it on the pumpkin, whip in the fluffy egg whites.

Heat the frying oil (a mix of olive and peanut oils is best, but an ordinary lightly aromatic olive oil will do). Cut the pumpkin into triangles ¼ to ½ inch thick.

In a broad soup plate, mix 2 tablespoons of sugar with the cinnamon and the finely grated orange and lemon peels. Roll the pumpkin pieces in this and then dip them in the batter. Place them in the hot oil. Brown the pieces on both sides before laying them on absorbent paper to drain. Be sure the oil is not too hot. The pumpkin needs to be thoroughly cooked when the dough is browned.

Serve the fritters hot and crusty, sprinkled with confectioners' sugar.

Apricot pizza

Pizza aux abricots

Serves 4

10 oz. (300 g) bread
dough
12 large apricots
½ tablespoon refined
flour

1 tablespoon ground
almonds
3 tablespoons sugar
2 tablespoons Nyons
olive oil

*Sweet and well-balanced with a hint of almonds,
Nyons olive oil accentuates the flavor of the apricots.*

Roll out the bread dough and place it on a
baking sheet.

In a bowl, mix 1 tablespoon of sugar, the ground
almonds and the refined flour. Spread over the dough.

Halve the apricots and remove the pits. Lay over
the dough. Sprinkle on 1 tablespoon of sugar
and 1 tablespoon of oil. Let the dough rise for 15
minutes at room temperature.

Put the sheet over a high heat for 2 minutes
to brown the bottom and make the dough rise a bit.
Place in an oven preheated to 400 °F for 10 minutes.

Just after taking the pizza out of the oven,
add a dash of olive oil and sprinkle 1 tablespoon
of sugar. Serve immediately.

Crêpes with rose water and honey
Crêpes à l'eau de rose et au miel

Serves 4	1²/3 cups milk	1/3 tablespoon flour	*honey sauce*
	2 tablespoons Provence olive oil	1/3 tablespoon corn starch	1 tablespoon Provence honey
crêpe batter	1/2 pod vanilla	1 cup milk	juice of 1/2 lemon
7 oz. (200 g) flour		2 tablespoons Provence olive oil	6 tablespoons water
3 eggs	*pastry cream*	1/4 pod vanilla	1/3 tablespoon butter
1 teaspoon salt	2 eggs	1/2 teaspoon rose water	1 tablespoon Provence olive oil
1³/4 oz. (50 g) sugar	1³/4 oz. (50 g) sugar		

Undertones of almond, flowers and honey make olive oil from the Massif de l'Esterel in Provence an ideal complement for this dessert.

Batter

Mix the flour with the salt, sugar, eggs and the scraped interior of vanilla pod (use the tip of a knife). Add the oil and milk. Beat well. Leave to rest for 1 hour in a cool place.

Pastry cream

Work the egg yolks with the sugar until the mix whitens. Add the corn starch and flour. Split the vanilla pod and add it to the milk. Heat over a low heat. Little by little, whipping the while with a whisk, pour in the egg and sugar mix. Continue whipping until the mix thickens. Add the oil.

Honey sauce

In a small pan, warm the honey until liquid. Add the rose water and lemon juice, oil, butter and water. Mix.

Grease a broad, flat pan with olive oil and heat. Pour on a thin layer of the crêpe batter for one crêpe at a time. Proceed as for pancakes until you have 4. Pour a bit of cream in the center of each crêpe. Fold in quarters and lay in a serving dish. Pour warm honey sauce over the crêpes and serve.

Swiss chard pie
Tourte aux blettes

Serves 4–6

crust
10 oz. (300 g) flour
4 oz. (120 g) butter
2 tablespoons Andalusian olive oil

1³/4 oz. (50 g) sugar
1 pinch salt

filling
12 oz. (350 g) Swiss chard leaves (stems removed)
9 oz. (250 g) Swiss chard stalks

3 tablespoons Provence honey
1¹/4 oz. (40 g) pine nuts
1¹/4 oz. (40 g) rum-soaked raisins
1¹/4 oz. (40 g) crushed almonds
1 tablespoon pastis

1 egg
3 tablespoons heavy cream
5 tablespoons Andalusian olive oil

Andalusian olive oil creates a fine blend of sweetness and vigor.

Crust

Mix all the ingredients. Work the dough with the fingertips, adding a bit of water until you get a supple and homogenous dough. Roll it in plastic or paper wrap and let it rest for 30 minutes in a cool place.

Filling

Wash and slice the Swiss chard stalks widthwise. Boil in salted water. After 5 minutes, add the washed greens. Cook 5 minutes. Thoroughly drain. Chop rather fine.

Cook the raisins for a few minutes with the rum and a bit of water. Reduce until dry. In a frying pan, brown the pine nuts in 1 tablespoon of olive oil. Add the raisins. Remove from the heat.

In a salad bowl, mix the egg with 4 tablespoons of oil and the cream, honey, crushed almond, pastis, pine nuts and raisins. Add the Swiss chard. Roll out the dough in two parts of about 10 inches each. Put one in the bottom of a buttered and floured pie pan and cover it with the filling. Cover that with the second piece of dough. Seal the edges by squeezing them together with dampened fingers. Make a hole in the center. Put it into an oven heated to 350 °F for 30 minutes. Serve cold.

Sherbet with basil and orange sauce, olive oil and candied olives

Sorbet à l'orange sauce basilic, huile d'olive et olives confites

Serves 4

sherbet
3 cups freshly pressed orange juice
1 cup freshly pressed lemon juice
3^1/2 oz. (100 g) sugar

basil and orange sauce
4/5 cup liquid cream
1 tablespoon sugar

3 branches basil
2 tablespoons Andalusian olive oil
a few drops of water
a few drops orange blossom extract
a few drops lemon juice
1 knife tip corn starch dissolved in 1 tablespoon of water

candied olives
2^3/4 oz. (80 g) firm black olives, seeds removed
3^1/2 oz. (100 g) cup sugar
6^1/2 tablespoons water

Andalusian olive oil is fruity and strong but has no trace of tartness.

Candied olives

Make the evening before. Halve the olives. To desalt, blanch 2 or 3 times in boiling water. Drain. Make a syrup with the sugar and water. Put in the olives and cook for 15 minutes. Remove from the heat. Leave the olives to soak for 24 hours.

Sherbet

Mix the ingredients in a sherbet (or ice-cream) maker. Ingredients can also be put in an ice container and left to freeze in a freezer. Remove the sherbet from the container by scraping with a fork.

Basil and orange sauce

Boil the cream and sugar together. Whip in the corn starch. Remove from the heat. Whip in 1 tablespoon of olive oil. Remove the basil leaves from the branches, shred and add. Leave to infuse and cool. Add the orange water and lemon juice.

Pour this sauce into 4 soup plates. Lay on scoops of sherbet. Sprinkle on the drained candied olives. Top with a basil leaf, add a dash of oil and serve immediately.

Fresh tomatoes and berries
Fraîcheur de tomate et fruits rouges

Serves 4

5 medium-size tomatoes, about 1 lb. 2 oz. (500 g) 1 lb. 2 oz. (500 g) raspberries, blackberries, red currants, wild and cultivated strawberries or other berries, according to season
2 tablespoons Andalusian olive oil
1 teaspoon balsam vinegar
2³⁄4 oz. (80 g) sugar
1 teaspoon tomato concentrate
3 turns black pepper from pepper mill
a few fresh mint leaves

A strength and generosity that echoes its native sunshine makes Andalusian olive oil an excellent complement for this summery dessert.

Rapidly wash and hull the strawberries. Remove the seeds from the tomatoes. Quarter 3 of them.

In a mixer, put 3 quartererd tomatoes, 1/4 lb. berries, 2 1/4 oz. sugar, the tomato concentrate, pepper, vinegar, olive oil and 4/5 cup water. Blend at high speed for 1 minute. The result should be smooth. Strain finely and chill in the refrigerator for 1 or 2 hours or in the freezer for 15 minutes.

Cut the pulp of the 2 remaining tomatoes into small cubes. Sprinkle on the remaining sugar. Mix and let marinate for 15 minutes.

Put a portion of chilled fruit sauce in 4 bowls. Put the remaining 1/4 lb. berries and diced tomatoes on top. Decorate with the mint. Serve chilled.

Madeleines with lavender flowers

Madeleines aux fleurs de lavande

Makes 12 madeleines

4³/4 oz. (140 g) sugar
4¹/2 oz. (130 g) flour
2 egg yolks
3 eggs

1 pinch salt
1 teaspoon baking soda
3¹/2 oz. (100 g) clarified butter
1 tablespoon Haute-Provence olive oil

¹/2 tablespoon chopped dried lavender blossoms

Haute-Provence oil has a sweet, refined savor and a bouquet of honey and almonds.

Clarify the butter by heating it in a small pan and removing the foam on the surface with a spoon.

Use a spatula to mix together (not whip) the 3 whole eggs and 2 yolks with the sugar, flour, salt and baking powder. Add the butter (which should be just barely warm and still liquid), olive oil and lavender.

Pour the batter into buttered and floured biscuit molds. Chill for 30 minutes in the refrigerator. Bake at 350 °F for about 15 minutes. Remove the madeleines from the molds and leave them to cool on their sides.

Dried fruit crisps with orange blossom scent
Croustillants de fruits secs à la fleur d'oranger

Makes 12 pastries

2 sheets of filo dough,
12–16 inches each
2 tablespoons Provence
honey

6 tablespoons Galilean
olive oil
2/3 oz. (20 g) hazel nuts
2/3 oz. (20 g) flaked
almonds

2/3 oz. (20 g) half-shelled
walnuts
2/3 oz. (20 g) pistachios
2/3 oz. (20 g) pine nuts
2/3 oz. (20 g) raisins
2/3 oz. (20 g) dried figs

2/3 oz. (20 g) candied
orange peel
a few drops of orange
extract

The light and lively savor of Galilean olive oil has a hint of honey.

Brown the nuts in 1 tablespoon of oil, adding the almonds last. Crush them in a mixer or food processor and put them back in the frying pan in 2 tablespoons of oil. Add the raisins, figs, chopped orange peel and 1 tablespoon of honey.

In a small saucepan, melt 1 tablespoon of honey with 3 tablespoons of olive oil and a few drops of orange extract. Brush this sauce over the top of one of the sheets of filo dough. Put the other sheet on top. Cut the double dough into 12 4-inch squares. Place a little ball of the nut-fruit mix on each square. Fold the dough over to cover. Brown for 5–6 minutes in an oven heated to 400 °F.

Connoisseur's Guide

THE WORLD'S FINEST OLIVE OILS

FRANCE

PRODUCTION: 2,400 tons of oil.

Haute-Provence

96 *communes*; 300,000 trees; 3,000 growers.

VARIETIES: Principally Aglandau, but also Picholine and Bouteillan.

OILS: Thick, savory and fruity. Vary according to locality. The oils from Manosque and Les Mées are the strongest in France.

USES: White meats, lamb, fish, pumpkin, baked vegetables.

Massif des Maures and Haut-Var

VARIETIES: Grossane, Aglandau, Picholine, Bouteillan and many others, some of which, such as Ribiers, are quite old.

OILS: Slightly spicy aroma with bouquets of white-fleshed fruits. Flavors vary, but generally rather sweet.

USES: Bouillabaisse, stream fish, sea bream and other grilled fish, grilled lamb, salads with nuts, including pine nuts.

Massif de l'Esterel and Nice Region

VARIETIES: Cailletier.

OILS: Pale yellow. Almond, hawthorn and acacia bouquets. Refined, sweet flavor.

Les Baux

VARIETIES: Grossane, Aglandau, Saloneque and Picholine.

OILS: Aromas of white flowers, bitter almond and pear. Full in the mouth.

USES: Lobster, bass, skate, fresh pasta, white meats, cooked vegetables.

Nyons (AOC)

VARIETIES: Tanche.

OILS: Bouquets of hazelnut and almonds. Flavor sweet and milky.

USES: Freshwater fish, white tuna, salads, summer fruit pies and other desserts.

Aix-en-Provence Region

77 *communes*; 270,000 trees

VARIETIES: Aglandau.

OILS: Green tomato, almond and hazelnut on the nose. Sharp and solid in the mouth with a touch of bitterness.

USES: All strong grilled fish, chopped chicken, raw or steamed vegetables.

Aude and Gard

VARIETIES: Principally Lucques, but also Picholine and other varieties.

OILS: Fruity and well-balanced.

Ardèche

VARIETIES: Principally Rougette.

OILS: Distinctive delicate woodland fruit aromas. Characteristic varietal flavors.

Corsica

VARIETIES: Principally Sabina, but also Picholine.

OILS: Herbal and vegetable perfumes. Full in the mouth. A bit green and fiery. Winter harvest oils are slightly bitter, while spring oils are sweeter.

USES: Carpaccio, gazpacho, Berber cooking, couscous, tajines, potato purée.

SPAIN

PRODUCTION: 970,000 tons, world's leading producer.

Andalusia

75% of Spain's production.

VARIETIES: Picual, Picudo, Hojiblanca, Lechin, Verdial, Ocal and others.

OILS: Very diverse flavors from one variety to the next and from one region to the next. For instance, Picudo oils from the Sierra Subbetica region can be citrusy, smooth and almost sugary.

Baena (small village near Cordoba)

VARIETIES: Picual, Picudo, Hojiblanca and others.

OILS: Floral bouquets. Fruity with a hint of spiciness and bitterness. Exceptional balance which is difficult to obtain.

USES: Lean fish, dishes with lemon or orange bases, spicy dishes, sweet and sour dishes, pastry doughs.

Sierra de Segura Region

VARIETIES: Picual, Hojiblanca.

OILS: Nicely aromatic, sometimes with an attractive hint of spiciness.

Priego de Cordoba (*between Granada and Cordoba*)
VARIETIES: Picual (also called Martena), Picudo, Hojiblanca.

OILS: Yellow with glints of green. Thick, fruity and fresh, with a touch of bitterness.

Sierra Magina Region
VARIETIES: Picual, Picudo, Hojiblanca, Lechin, Verdial, Ocal and others.

OILS: Fruity and strong but very well balanced.

Castille and Mancha
Major modern production.

VARIETIES: Cornicabra.

OIL: Distinctive, ripe and very aromatic. Often bitter and sometimes with a bite.

Aragon
VARIETIES: Empeltre.

OILS: Golden color. Fruity and sweet, with bouquets reminiscent of apples.

Estremadura
6% of Spain's production.

VARIETIES: Cornicabra, Carasquena and Morsica.

OILS: Strong and wild.

Catalonia
Les Garrigues (Larida Region)

VARIETIES: Principally Arbequina, but also some Fraga and Empeltre.

OILS: Rather fruity and lively but sweet, smooth and refined, with a hint of almonds, milk and toasted bread.

USES: Sole, mullet, meats, cheeses.

Siurana Region (in Tarragon)
VARIETIES: Arbequina.

OILS: Pale yellow and very sweet.

ITALY

PRODUCTION: 420,000 tons.

Tuscany
VARIETIES: Frantoio, Leccino, Moraiolo, Olivastra, Pendolino and others.

OILS: In the region of Lucca, yellow, light and fluid; in Chianti, green highlights, spicy with hints of artichoke and pepper; in Montalcino, deep colors, rustic and intense flavors.

USES: Smaller raw and cooked vegetables, especially broccoli, and cold pork, grilled fish and pasta.

Umbria
VARIETIES: Frantoio, Leccino, Moraiolo, Agogia, Raggiola.

OILS: Artichoke and green tomato bouquets with a hint of hot pepper. Slightly fruity flavor. Silky and lively.

Campagna
VARIETIES: Frantoio, Leccino, Carolea, Coratina, Ogliarota.

OILS: Golden color. Thick and fruity.

Liguria
VARIETIES: Taggiasca, Opalino and others.

OILS: Sweet and delicate.

Latium
VARIETIES: Frantoio.

OILS: Intense but refined. Mineral savor.

USES: Turbot, grilled bream, spider crab, rock lobster, pasta, tomatoes, fresh Brousse cheese.

Calabria
VARIETIES: Carolea, Nocellara and others

OILS: Fruity and quite vegetal with a hint of bitterness.

Puglia
Almost half of Italian production.

VARIETIES: Coratina, Provenzale, Ogliarola and others.

OILS: In the Bari region, very fruity and light; in Bitonto, fruity and light, close to the taste of fresh olives with a sweet almond savor; in general, vegetal bouquets of straw and white-flesh fruits.

USES: Cooked and raw green vegetables.

Sicily
VARIETIES: Biancolilla, Moresca, Cerasuola, Nocellara, Tonda Iblea.

OILS: From the coast, intense flavors with a touch of sweet almond; from around Ragusa, body and fruitiness; from the heights, rounded and very fruity.

USES: Seafoods and green vegetables, fish marinated with lemon.

Sardinia
VARIETIES: Bianca, Tonda, Bosana and others.

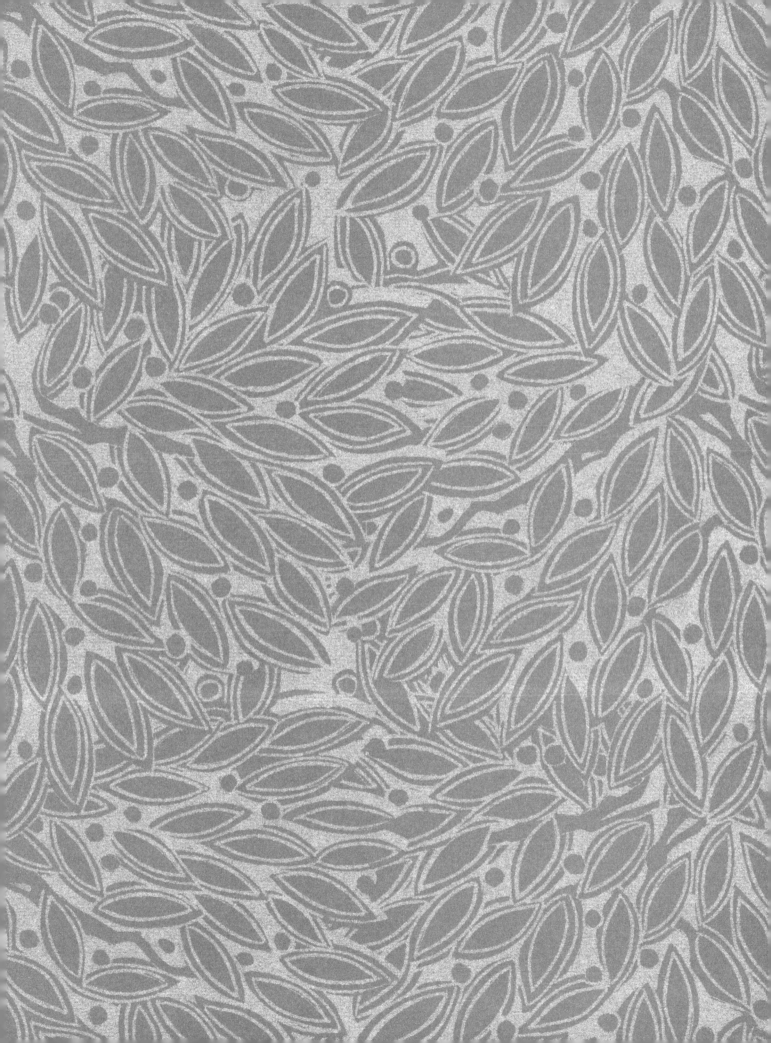

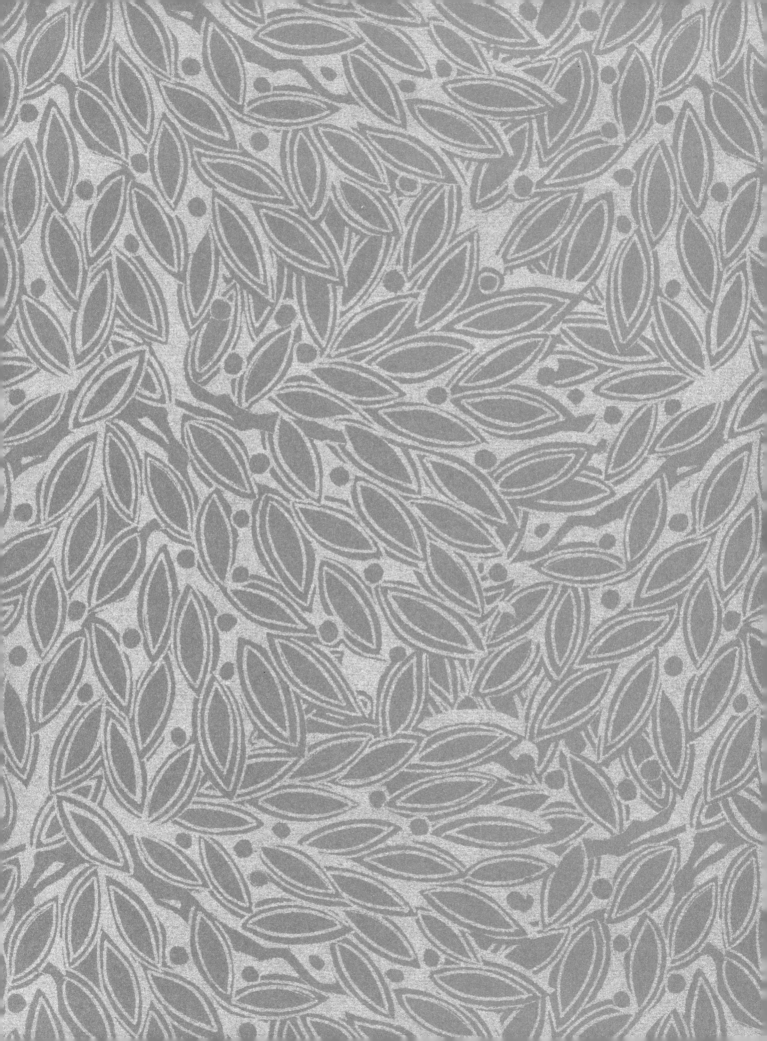